Thomas Stothard, Thomas Day

The History of Sandford and Merton - A work Intended for the Use of Children

Vol. III

Thomas Stothard, Thomas Day

The History of Sandford and Merton - A work Intended for the Use of Children
Vol. III

ISBN/EAN: 9783337225506

Printed in Europe, USA, Canada, Australia, Japan

Cover: Foto ©ninafisch / pixelio.de

More available books at **www.hansebooks.com**

THE HISTORY OF SANDFORD AND MERTON,

A WORK

Intended for the Use of CHILDREN.

Let not, O generous youth! thy mind recoil
At transitory pain, or manly toil!
Nor fondly linger in the painted vale,
Nor crop the flowers, nor woo the summer's gale!
Heedless of pleasure's voice, be thine the care
Nobly to suffer and sublimely dare!
While virtue waves on high her radiant prize,
And each hard step but lifts thee to the skies.

IN THREE VOLUMES.

VOL. III.

THE SEVENTH EDITION CORRECTED.

EMBELLISHED WITH FRONTISPIECES.

LONDON:
PRINTED FOR JOHN STOCKDALE, PICCADILLY
1795.

THE HISTORY OF SANDFORD AND MERTON.

WHILE these scenes were passing, Mrs. Merton, though ignorant of the danger of her son, was not undisturbed at home. Some accounts had been brought of Harry's combat, which served to make her uneasy and to influence her still more against him. Mrs. Compton too and Miss Matilda, who had conceived a violent dislike to Harry, were busy to inflame her by their malicious representations. While she was in these dispositions Mr. Merton happened to enter, and was at once attacked by all the ladies upon the subject of this improper connection. He endeavoured, for a long time, to remove their prejudices by reason, but when he found that to be impossible, he contented himself with telling his wife, that a little time would perhaps decide which were the most proper companions for their son; and that till Harry had done something to render himself unworthy of their notice he never could consent to the treating him with coldness or neglect. At this moment a female servant burst into the room with all the wildness of affright, and cried out with a voice that was scarcely articulate, Oh! madam, madam! such an accident—poor, dear master Tommy..... What of him, for God's sake? cried out Mrs. Merton, with an impatience and concern that sufficiently marked her feelings. Nay, madam, answered the servant, he is not much hurt they say: but little Sandford has taken him to a bullbaiting, and the bull has gored him, and William and John are bringing him home in their arms. These words were scarcely delivered when Mrs. Merton uttered a violent shriek, and was instantly seized with an hysteric fit. While the ladies were all employed in assisting her and restoring her senses, Mr. Merton, who, though much alarmed,

alarmed, was more composed, walked precipitately out, to learn the truth of this imperfect narration. He had not proceeded far, before he met the crowd of children and servants, one of whom carried Tommy Merton in his arms. As soon as he was convinced that his son had received no other damage than a violent fright, he began to inquire into the circumstances of the affair, but before he had time to receive any information, Mrs. Merton, who had recovered from her fainting, came running wildly from the house. When she saw that her son was safe, she caught him in her arms, and began to utter all the incoherent expressions of a mother's fondness. It was with difficulty that her husband could prevail upon her to moderate her transports till they were within. Then she gave a loose to her feelings in all their violence; and, for a considerable time, was incapable of attending to any thing but the joy of his miraculous preservation. At length, however, she became more composed, and observing that all the company were present except Harry Sandford, she exclaimed with sudden indignation; So, I see that little abominable wretch has not had the impudence to follow you in: and I almost wish that the bull had gored him as he deserved. What little wretch, mamma, said Tommy, do you mean? Whom can I mean, cried Mrs. Merton, but that vile Harry Sandford, that your father is so fond of, and who had nearly cost you your life by leading you into this danger? He! mamma, said Tommy, he lead me into danger! He did all he could to persuade me not to go; and I was a very naughty boy indeed, not to take his advice. Mrs. Merton stood amazed at this information; for her prejudices had operated so powerfully upon her mind, that she had implicitly believed the guilt of Harry upon the imperfect evidence of the maid. Who was it then, said Mr. Merton, could be so imprudent? Indeed, papa, answered Tommy, we were all to blame, all but Harry, who advised and begged us not to go, and particularly me, because he said it would give you so much uneasiness when you knew it, and that it was so dangerous a diversion. Mrs. Merton looked confused at her mistake, but Mrs. Compton observed that she supposed Harry was afraid of the danger, and therefore had wisely kept out of the way. Oh! no, indeed, madam, answered one of the little boys; Harry is no coward, though we thought him so at first, when he

let

let master Tommy strike him; but he fought Master Mash in the bravest manner I ever saw, and though Master Mash fought very well, yet Harry had the advantage; and I saw him follow us at a little distance, and keep his eye upon Master Merton all the time, till the bull broke loose; and then I was so frightened that I do not know what became of him. So, this is the little boy, said Mr. Merton, that you were for driving from the society of your children! But let us hear more of the story, for as yet I know neither the particulars of his danger nor his escape. Upon this, one of the servants, who from some little distance had seen the whole affair, was called in and examined. He gave them an exact account of all; of Tommy's misfortune; of Harry's bravery; of the unexpected succour of the poor black; and filled the whole room with admiration that such an action, so noble, so intrepid, so fortunate, should have been atchieved by such a child.

Mrs. Merton was now silent with shame at reflecting upon her own unjust prejudices, and the ease with which she had become the enemy of a boy who had saved the life of her darling son; and who appeared as much superior in character to all the young
gentle-

gentlemen at her houfe, as they exceeded him in rank and fortune. The young ladies now forgot their former objections to his perfon and manners, and fuch is the effect of genuine virtue, all the company confpired to extol the conduct of Harry to the fkies. But Mr. Merton, who had appeared more delighted than all the reft with the relation of Harry's intrepidity, now caft his eyes around the room, and feemed to be looking for his little friend. But when he could not find him, he faid, with fome concern, Where can be our little deliverer? Sure he can have met with no accident that he has not returned with the reft! No, faid one of the fervants, as to that, Harry Sandford is fafe enough, for I faw him go towards his own home in company with the black. Alas! anfwered Mr. Merton, furely he muft have received fome unworthy treatment that could make him thus abruptly defert us all. And now I recollect that I heard one of the young gentlemen mention a blow that Harry had received; furely, Tommy, you could not have been fo bafely ungrateful as to ftrike the beft and nobleft of your friends! Tommy, at this, hung down his head; his face was covered with a burning blufh, and the tears began

silently

silently to trickle down his cheeks. Mrs. Merton remarked the anguish and confusion of her child, and, catching him in her arms, was going to clasp him to her bosom with the most endearing expressions; but Mr. Merton, hastily interrupting her, said, It is not now a time to give way to fondness for a child, that, I fear, has acted the basest and vilest part that can disgrace an human being; and who, if what I suspect is true, can be only a dishonour to his parents. At this Tommy could no longer contain himself, but burst out into such a violent transport of crying, that Mrs. Merton, who seemed to feel the severity of Mr. Merton's conduct with still more poignancy than her son, caught her darling up in her arms, and carried him abruptly out of the room, accompanied by most of the ladies, who pitied Tommy's abasement, and agreed that there was no crime he could have been guilty of which was not amply atoned for by such a charming sensibility.

But Mr. Merton, who now felt all the painful interest of a tender father, and considered this as the critical moment which was to give his son the impression of worth or baseness for life, was determined to examine the affair to the utmost. He therefore took the first opportunity of drawing the little boy aside who had mentioned master Merton's striking Harry, and questioned him upon the subject. But he, who had no particular interest in disguising the truth, related the circumstances nearly as they had happened; and, though he a little softened matters in Tommy's favour, yet, without intending it, he held up such a picture of his violence and injustice as wounded his father to the soul. While Mr. Merton was occupied by these uneasy feelings, he was agreeably surprized by a visit from Mr. Barlow, who came accidentally to see him, with a perfect ignorance of all the great events which had so recently happened. Mr. Merton received this worthy man with the sincerest cordiality; but there was such a gloom diffused over all his manners, that Mr. Barlow began to suspect that all was not right with Tommy, and therefore purposely inquired after him, to give his father an opportunity of speaking. This Mr. Merton did not fail to do; and taking Mr. Barlow affectionately by the hand, he said, Oh! my dear sir, I begin to fear that all my hopes are at an end in that boy, and all your kind endeavours thrown away. He has just behaved in such a manner as shews him

him to be radically corrupted, and infenfible of every principle but pride. He then related to Mr. Barlow every incident of Tommy's behaviour, making the fevereft reflections upon his infolence and ingratitude, and blaming his own fupinenefs that had not earlier checked thefe boifterous paffions, that now burft forth with fuch a degree of fury and threatened ruin to his hopes. Indeed, anfwered Mr. Barlow, I am very forry to hear this account of my little friend; yet, I do not fee it quite in fo ferious a light as yourfelf: and, though I cannot deny the dangers that may arife from a character fo fufceptible of falfe impreffions, and fo violent at the fame time, yet I do not think the corruption either fo great, or fo general, as you feem to fufpect. Do we not fee, even in the moft trifling habits of body or fpeech, that a long and continual attention is required, if we would wifh to change them; and yet our perfeverance is in the end generally fuccefsful? Why then fhould we imagine that thofe of the mind are lefs obftinate, or fubject to different laws? Or, why fhould we rafhly abandon ourfelves to defpair, from the firft experiments that do not fucceed according to our wifhes? Indeed, anfwered Mr. Merton, what you say is perfectly confiftent with the general benevolence of your character; and moft confolatory to the tendernefs of a father. Yet, I know too well the general weaknefs of parents in refpect to the faults of their children, not to be upon my guard againft the delufions of my own mind. And when I confider the abrupt tranfition of my fon into every thing that is moft inconfiftent with goodnefs; how lightly, how inftantaneoufly he feems to have forgotten every thing he had learned with you, I cannot help forming the moft painful and melancholy prefages of the future. Alas, fir, anfwered Mr. Barlow, what is the general malady of human nature but this very inftability which now appears in your fon? Do you imagine that half the vices of men arife from real depravity of heart? On the contrary, I am convinced that human nature is infinitely more weak than wicked; and that the greater part of all bad conduct fprings rather from want of firmnefs than from any fettled propenfity to evil. Indeed, replied Mr. Merton, what you fay is highly reafonable; nor did I ever expect that a boy fo long indulged and fpoiled fhould be exempt from failings. But what particularly hurts me is, to fee him proceed to fuch disagreeable extremities without any adequate temptation; extremities that I fear imply a defect of goodness and generosity, virtues which I always thought he had possessed in a very great degree. Neither, answered Mr. Barlow, am I at all convinced that your son is deficient in either. But you are to consider the prevalence of example, and the circle to which you have lately introduced him. If it is so difficult even for persons of a more mature age and experience to resist the impressions of those with whom they constantly associate, how can you expect it from your son? To be armed against the prejudices of the world, and to distinguish real merit from the splendid vices which pass current in what is called society, is one of the most difficult of human sciences. Nor do I know a single character, however excellent, that would not candidly confess he has often made a wrong election, and paid that homage to a brilliant outside which is only due to real merit. You comfort me very much, said Mr. Merton, but such ungovernable passions! such violence and impetuosity!—Are indeed very formidable, replied Mr. Barlow. Yet, when they are properly directed, frequently produce the noblest effects; and history,

history, as well as private observation, may inform us, that, if they sometimes lead their possessor astray, they are equally capable of bringing him back to the right path, provided they are properly acted upon. You have, I doubt not, read the story of Polemo, who, from a debauched young man, became a celebrated philosopher, and a model of virtue, only by attending a single moral lecture. Indeed, said Mr. Merton, I am ashamed to confess that the various employments and amusements in which I have passed the greater part of my life, have not afforded me as much leisure for reading as I could wish. You will therefore oblige me very much by repeating the story you allude to.

The Story of Polemo.

Polemo, said Mr. Barlow, was a young man of Athens, so distinguished by his excesses, that he was the aversion of all the discreter part of the city. He led a life of continual intemperance and dissipation. His days were given up to feasting and amusements, his nights to riot and intoxication. He was constantly surrounded by a set of loose young men who imitated and
en-

encouraged his vices; and when they had totally drowned the little reason they possest, in copious draughts of wine, they were accustomed to sally out, and practise every species of absurd and licentious frolic. One morning they were thus wandering about, after having spent the night as usual, when they beheld a great concourse of people that were listening to the discourses of a celebrated philosopher named Xenocrates. The greater part of the young men, who still retained some sense of shame, were so struck with this spectacle, that they turned out of the way, but Polemo, who was more daring and abandoned than the rest, pressed forward into the midst of the audience. His figure was too remarkable not to attract universal notice; for his head was crowned with flowers, his robe hung negligently about him, and his whole body was reeking with perfumes; besides, his look and manners were such as very little qualified him for such a company. Many of the audience were so displeased at this interruption, that they were ready to treat the young man with great severity, but the venerable philosopher prevailed upon them not to molest the intruder, and calmly continued his discourse, which happened to be upon the dignity and

advantage

advantage of temperance. As he proceeded, he descanted upon this subject with so much force and eloquence, that the young man became more composed and attentive, as it were, in spite of himself. Presently, as the sage grew still more animated in his representation of the shameful slavery which attends the giving way to our passions, and the sublime happiness of reducing them all to order, the countenance of Polemo began to change, and the expression of it to be softened. He cast his eyes in mournful silence upon the ground, as if in deep repentance for his own contemptible conduct. Still the philosopher increased in vehemence; he seemed to be animated with the sacred genius of the art which he profest, and to exercise an irresistible power over the minds of his hearers. He drew the portrait of an ingenuous and modest young man, that had been bred up to virtuous toils and manly hardiness. He painted him triumphant over all his passions, and trampling upon human fears and weakness. Should his country be invaded, you see him fly to its defence, and ready to pour forth all his blood. Calm and composed he appears with a terrible beauty in the front of danger, the ornament and bulwark of

of his country. The thickeft fquadrons are penetrated by his refiftlefs valour, and he points the paths of victory to his admiring followers. Should he fall in battle, how glorious is his lot! to be cut off in the honourable difcharge of his duty, to be wept by all the brave and virtuous, and to furvive in the eternal records of fame!——
While Xenocrates was thus difcourfing, Polemo feemed to be tranfported with a facred enthufiafm; his eyes flafhed fire, his countenance glowed with martial indignation, and the whole expreffion of his perfon was changed. Prefently, the philofopher, who had remarked the effects of his difcourfe, painted in no lefs glowing colours the life and manners of an effeminate young man. Unhappy youth, faid he, what words fhall I find equal to thy abafement? Thou art the reproach of thy parents, the difgrace of thy country, the fcorn or pity of every generous mind. How is nature difhonoured in thy perfon, and all her choiceft gifts abortive! That ftrength which would have rendered thee the glory of thy city, and the terror of her foes, is bafely thrown away on luxury and intemperance! thy youth and beauty are wafted in riot and prematurely blafted by difeafe. Inftead of the eye of fire, the port of intrepidity,

the

the step of modest firmness, a squalid paleness sits upon thy face, a bloated corpulency enfeebles thy limbs, and presents a picture of human nature in its most abject state. But hark! the trumpet sounds; a savage band of unrelenting enemies have surrounded the city, and are prepared to scatter flames and ruin through the whole! The virtuous youth that have been educated to nobler cares, arm with generous emulation, and fly to its defence. How lovely do they appear, drest in resplendent arms, and moving slowly on in a close, impenetrable phalanx! They are animated by every motive which can give energy to an human breast, and lift it to the sublimest atchievements. Their hoary sires, their venerable magistrates, the beauteous forms of trembling virgins, attend them to the war, with prayers and acclamations. Go forth, ye generous bands, secure to meet the rewards of victory, or the repose of honourable death! Go forth, ye generous bands, but unaccompanied by the wretch I have described. His feeble arm refuses to bear the ponderous shield; the pointed spear sinks feebly from his grasp; he trembles at the noise and tumult of the war, and flies like the hunted hart to lurk in shades and darkness.

nefs. Behold him rouzed from his midnight orgies, reeking with wine and odours, and crowned with flowers, the only trophies of his warfare; he hurries with trembling steps acrofs the city; his voice, his gait, his whole deportment proclaim the abject flave of intemperance, and ftamp indelible infamy upon his name. While Xenocrates was thus difcourfing, Polemo liftened with fixt attention: the former animation of his countenance gave way to a vifible dejection; prefently his lips trembled and his cheeks grew pale; he was loft in melancholy recollection, and a filent tear was obferved to trickle down. But when the philofopher defcribed a character fo like his own, fhame feemed to take intire poffeffion of his foul, and rouzing, as from a long and painful lethargy, he foftly raifed his hands to his head, and tore away the chaplets of flowers, the monuments of his effeminacy and difgrace: he feemed intent to compofe his drefs into a more decent form, and wrapped his robe about him, that before hung loofely waving with an air of ftudied effeminacy. But when Xenocrates had finifhed his difcourfe, Polemo approached him with all the humility of confcious guilt, and begged to become his difciple; telling him that he had

had that day gained the moſt glorious conqueſt that had ever been atchieved by reaſon and philoſophy, by inſpiring with the love of virtue a mind that had been hitherto plunged in folly and ſenſuality. Xenocrates embraced the young man, encouraged him in ſuch a laudable deſign, and admitted him among his diſciples. Nor had he ever reaſon to repent of his facility, for Polemo from that hour abandoned all his former companions and vices, and by his uncommon ardor for improvement, very ſoon became as celebrated for virtue and wiſdom as he had before been for every contrary quality.

Thus, added Mr. Barlow, you ſee how little reaſon there is to deſpair of youth, even in the moſt diſadvantageous circumſtances. It has been juſtly obſerved that few know all they are capable of; the ſeeds of different qualities frequently lie concealed in the character, and only wait for an opportunity of exerting themſelves; and it is the great buſineſs of education to apply ſuch motives to the imagination, as may ſtimulate it to laudable exertions. For thus the ſame activity of mind, the ſame impetuoſity of temper, which, by being improperly applied, would only form a wild, un-
govern-

governable character, may produce the steadiest virtue, and prove a blessing both to the individual and his country.

I am infinitely obliged to you for this story, said Mr. Merton, and as my son will certainly find a Xenocrates in you, I wish that you may have reason to think him in some degree a Polemo. But, since you are so kind as to present me with these agreeable hopes, do not leave the work unfinished, but tell me what you think the best method of treating him in his present critical situation. That, said Mr. Barlow, must depend, I think, upon the workings of his own mind. He has always appeared to me generous and humane, and to have a fund of natural goodness amid all the faults which spring up too luxuriantly in his character. It is impossible that he should not be at present possest with the keenest shame for his own behaviour. It will be your first part to take advantage of these sentiments, and, instead of a fleeting and transitory sensation, to change them into fixt and active principles. Do not at present say much to him upon the subject. Let us both be attentive to the silent workings of his mind, and regulate our behaviour accordingly.

This

This conversation being finished, Mr. Merton introduced Mr. Barlow to the company in the other room. Mrs. Merton, who now began to be a little staggered in some of the opinions she had been most fond of, received him with uncommon civility, and all the rest of the company treated him with the greatest respect. But Tommy, who had lately been the oracle and the admiration of all this brilliant circle, appeared to have lost all his vivacity. He indeed advanced to meet Mr. Barlow with a look of tenderness and gratitude, and made the most respectful answers to all his inquiries; but his eyes were involuntarily turned to the ground, and silent melancholy and dejection were visible in his face. Mr. Barlow remarked with the greatest pleasure these signs of humility and contrition, and pointed them out to Mr. Merton the first time he had an opportunity of speaking to him without being overheard; adding, that unless he was much deceived, Tommy would soon give ample proofs of the natural goodness of his character, and reconcile himself to all his friends. Mr. Merton heard this observation with the greatest pleasure, and now began to entertain some hopes of seeing it accomplished.

After

After the dinner was over, most of the young gentlemen went away to their respective homes. Tommy seemed to have lost much of the enthusiasm which he had lately felt for his polite and accomplished friends; he even appeared to feel a secret joy at their departure, and answered with a visible coldness all their professions of regard and repeated invitations. Even Mrs. Compton herself and Miss Matilda, who were also departing, found him as insensible as the rest; though they did not spare the most extravagant praises and the warmest professions of regard.

And now the ceremonies of taking leave being over, and most of the visitors departed, a sudden solitude seemed to have taken possession of the house which was lately the seat of noise, and bustle, and festivity. Mr. and Mrs. Merton and Mr. Barlow were left alone with Miss Simmons and Tommy, and one or two others of the smaller gentry who had not yet returned to their friends. As Mr. Barlow was not fond of cards, Mr. Merton proposed, after the tea-table was removed, that Miss Simmons, who was famous for reading well, should entertain the company with some little tale or history, adapted to the comprehension even
of

of the youngest. Miss Simmons excused herself with the greatest modesty, but upon Mrs. Merton's joining in the request, she instantly complied, and fetching down a book, read the following story of

SOPHRON and TIGRANES.

Sophron and Tigranes were the children of two neighbouring shepherds that fed their flocks in that part of Asia which borders upon mount Lebanon. They were accustomed to each other from their earliest infancy, and the continual habit of conversing at length produced a tender and intimate friendship. Sophron was the larger and more robust of the two; his look was firm, but modest, his countenance placid, and his eyes were such as inspired confidence and attachment. He excelled most of the youth of the neighbourhood in every species of violent exercise, such as wrestling, boxing, and whirling heavy weights; but his triumphs were constantly mixed with so much humanity and courtesy, that even those who found themselves vanquished could feel no envy towards their conqueror. On the contrary, Tigranes was of a character totally different. His body was less strong than

than that of Sophron, but excellently proportioned, and adapted to every species of fatigue. His countenance was full of fire, but displeased by an excess of confidence; and his eyes sparkled with sense and meaning, but bore too great an expression of uncontrouled fierceness. Nor were these two youths less different in the application of their faculties than in the nature of them; for Tigranes seemed to be possessed by a restless spirit of commanding all his equals, while Sophron, contented with the enjoyment of tranquility, desired nothing more than to avoid oppression.

Still as they assisted their parents in leading every morning their flocks to pasture, they entertained each other with rural sports, or, laid under the shade of arching rocks, during the heat of the day, conversed with all the ease of childish friendship. Their observations were not many; they were chiefly drawn from the objects of nature which surrounded them, or from the simple modes of life to which they had been witness; but even here the diversity of their characters was sufficiently expressed. See, said Tigranes one day, as he cast his eyes upwards to the cliffs of a neighbouring rock, that eagle which rises into the immense

mense regions of air, till he absolutely soars beyond the reach of sight; were I a bird, I should choose to resemble him, that I might traverse the clouds with the rapidity of a whirlwind, and dart like lightning upon my prey. That eagle, answered Sophron, is the emblem of violence and injustice; he is the enemy of every bird, and even of every beast that is weaker than himself: were I to choose, I should prefer the life of yonder swan, that moves so smoothly and inoffensively along the river; he is strong enough to defend himself from injury, without oppressing others; and, therefore, he is neither feared nor insulted by other animals. While he was yet speaking, the eagle, who had been hovering in the air, darted suddenly down at some distance, and seizing a lamb, was bearing it away in his cruel talons; when, almost in the same instant, the shepherd, who had been watching all his motions from a neighbouring hill, let fly an arrow from his bow, with so unerring an aim that it pierced the body of the bird, and brought him headlong to the ground, writhing in the agonies of death. This, said Sophron, I have often heard is the fate of ambitious people; while they are endeavouring to mount beyond their fellows, they

are

are stopped by some unforeseen misfortune. For my part, said Tigranes, I had rather perish in the middle of the sky, than enjoy an age of life, basely chained down and grovelling upon the surface of the earth. What we either may enjoy, answered Sophron, is in the hand of Heaven; but may I rather creep, during life, than mount to commit injustice and oppress the innocent!

In this manner passed the early years of the two friends. As they grew up to manhood the difference of their tempers became more visible, and gradually alienated them from each other. Tigranes began to despise the uniform labours of a shepherd, and the humble occupations of the country. His sheep were neglected, and frequently wandered over the plains, without a leader to guard them in the day or bring them back at night. The young man was in the mean time employed in climbing rocks, or traversing the forest, to seek for eagles nests, or pierce with his arrows the different wild animals which inhabit the woods. If he heard the horn of the hunter, or the cry of hounds, it was impossible to restrain his eagerness. He regarded neither the summer's sun nor the winter's frost while he was pursuing his game. The thickest woods, the steepest mountains, the deepest rivers, were unable to stop him in his career. He triumphed over every danger and difficulty with such an invincible courage as made him at once an object of terror and admiration to all the youth in the neighbourhood. His friend Sophron alone beheld his exploits neither with terror nor admiration. Of all his comrades Sophron was the only one whom Tigranes still continued to respect, for he knew that, with a gentleness of temper which scarcely any thing could exasperate, he possessed the firmest courage, and a degree of bodily strength which rendered that courage invincible. He affected, indeed, to despise the virtuous moderation of his friend, and ridiculed it with some of his looser comrades as an abject pusillanimity; but he felt himself humbled whenever he was in his company as before a superior being, and therefore gradually estranged himself from his society.

Sophron, on the contrary, entertained the sincerest regard for his friend, but he knew his defects, and trembled for the consequences which the violence and ambition of his character might one day produce. Whenever Tigranes abandoned his flocks or left
his

his rustic tasks undone, Sophron had the goodness to supply whatever he had omitted. Such was the vigour of his constitution that he was indefatigable in every labour, nor did he ever exert his force more willingly than in performing these voluntary duties to his absent friend. Whenever he met with Tigranes, he accosted him in the gentlest manner, and endeavoured to win him back to his former habits and manners. He represented to him the injury he did his parents, and the disquietude he occasioned in their minds, by thus abandoning the duties of his profession. He sometimes, but with the greatest mildness, hinted at the coldness with which Tigranes treated him; and reminded his friend of the pleasing intercourse of their childhood. But all his remonstrances were vain; Tigranes heard him at first with coolness, then with impatience or contempt, and, at last, avoided him altogether.

Sophron had a lamb which he had formerly saved from the devouring jaws of a wolf, who had already bitten him in several places, and destroyed his dam. The tenderness with which this benevolent young man had nursed and fed him during his infancy had so attached him to his master, that he seemed to prefer his society to that of his own species. Wherever Sophron went, the faithful lamb accompanied him like his dogs, lay down beside him when he reposed, and followed close behind when he drove the rest of the flock to pasture. Sophron was equally attached to his dumb companion; he often diverted himself with his innocent gambols, fed him with the choicest herbs out of his hands, and when he slept at night, the lamb was sure to repose beside him.

It happened about this time, that Tigranes, as he was one day exploring the woods, discovered the den of a she-wolf, in which she had left her young ones while she went out to search for prey. By a caprice that was natural to his temper, he chose out the largest of the whelps, carried it home to his house, and brought it up as if it had been an useful and harmless animal. While it was yet but young, it was incapable of doing mischief; but as it increased in age and strength, it began to shew signs of a bloody and untameable disposition, and made all the neighbouring shepherds tremble for the safety of their flocks. But, as the courage and fierceness of Tigranes had now rendered him formidable to all his associates,

sociates, and the violence of his temper made him impatient of all opposition, they did not speak to him upon the subject; and as to his own parents, he had long learned to treat them with indifference or contempt. Sophron alone, who was not to be awed by fear, observing the just apprehensions of the neighbourhood, undertook the task of expostulating with his friend, and endeavoured to prevail upon him to part with a beast so justly odious, and which might in the end prove fatal whenever his natural rage should break out into open acts of slaughter. Tigranes heard him with a sneer of derision, and only answered; that, if a parcel of miserable rustics diverted themselves with keeping sheep, he, who had a more elevated soul, might surely entertain a nobler animal for his diversion. But, should that nobler animal prove a public mischief, coolly replied Sophron, you must expect that he will be treated as a public enemy. Woe be to the man, answered Tigranes, brandishing his javelin and sternly frowning, that shall dare to meddle with any thing that belongs to me! Saying this, he turned his back upon Sophron, and left him with disdain.

It was not long before the very event took place which had been so long foreseen.

The wolf of Tigranes, either impelled by the accidental taste of blood, or by the natural fierceness of his own temper, fell one day upon the sheep with such an unexpected degree of fury, that he slaughtered thirty of them before it was possible to prevent him. Sophron happened at that time to be within view; he ran with amazing swiftness to the place, and found the savage bathed in blood, tearing the carcase of a lamb which he had just slain. At the approach of the daring youth the wolf began to utter a dismal cry, and, quitting his prey, seemed to prepare himself for a slaughter of another kind. Sophron was entirely unarmed, and the size and fury of the beast which rushed forward to attack him might well have excused him had he declined the combat. But he, consulting only his native courage, wrapped his shepherd's cloak around his left arm to resist the first onset of his enemy, and, with a determined look and nimble pace, advanced towards his threatening adversary. In an instant the wolf sprang upon him, with an horrid yell; but Sophron nimbly eluded his attack, and, suddenly throwing his vigorous arms about the body of his adversary, compelled him to struggle for his own safety. It was then that he uttered

tered cries more dreadful than before; and as he writhed about in all the agitations of pain and madness, he gnashed his terrible teeth with impotent attempts to bite; while the blood and foam which issued from his jaws rendered his figure still more horrible than before. But Sophron, with undaunted courage, still maintained his hold, and, grasping him with irresistible strength, prevented him from using either his teeth or claws in his own defence. It was not long before the struggles and violence of the wolf grew perceptibly weaker from fatigue, and he seemed to wish to decline a farther combat with so formidable a foe, could he have found means to escape. Sophron then collected all his strength, and, seizing his fainting adversary by the neck and throat, grasped him still tighter in his terrible hands, till the beast, incapable either of disengaging himself or breathing, yielded up the contest and his life together. It was almost in this moment that Tigranes passed that way, and unexpectedly was witness to the triumphs of Sophron, and the miserable end of his favourite. Inflamed with pride and indignation, he uttered dreadful imprecations against his friend, who, in vain, attempted to explain the transaction; and,

rushing

rushing upon him with all the madness of inveterate hate, aimed a javelin at his bosom. Sophron was calm as he was brave; he saw the necessity of defending his own life against the attacks of a perfidious friend; and, with a nimble spring, at once eluded the weapon and closed with his antagonist. The combat was then more equal, for each was reduced to depend upon his own strength and activity. They struggled for some time with all the efforts which disappointed rage could inspire on the one side, and a virtuous indignation on the other. At length the fortune, or rather the force and coolness of Sophron, prevailed over the blind impetuous fury of Tigranes: he at once exerted his whole remaining strength with such success, that he hurled his adversary to the ground, where he lay bleeding, vanquished, and unable to rise. Thou scarcely, said Sophron, deservest thy life from my hands, who couldst so wantonly and unjustly attempt to deprive me of mine; however, I will rather remember thy early merits than thy recent injuries. No, replied the raging Tigranes, load me not with thy odious benefits, but rather rid me of a life which I abhor, since thou hast robbed me of my honour. I will never hurt thee, replied

plied Sophron, but in my own juſt defence; live to make a better uſe of life, and to have juſter ideas of honour. Saying this, he afſiſted Tigranes to riſe, but finding his temper full of implacable reſentment, he turned another way, and left him to go home alone.

It was not long after this event, that a company of ſoldiers marched acroſs the plains where Sophron was feeding his flocks, and halted to refreſh themſelves under the ſhade of ſome ſpreading trees. The officer who commauded them was ſtruck with the comely figure and expreſſive countenance of Sophron. He called the young man to him and endeavoured to inflame him with a military ardor, by ſetting before him the glory which might be acquired by arms, and ridiculing the obſcurity of a country life. When he thought he had ſufficiently excited his admiration, he propoſed to him that he ſhould enrol himſelf in his company, and promiſed him every encouragement which he thought moſt likely to engage the paſſions of a young man. Sophron thanked him with humility for his offers, but told him, that he had an aged father, who was now become incapable of maintaining himſelf; and therefore that he could accept

accept of no offers, however advantageous they might appear, which would interfere with the difcharge of his duty. The officer replied, and ridiculed the fcruples of the young man; but, finding him inflexible in his refolution, he at laft turned from him with an air of contempt, and called his men to follow him, muttering as he went reflections upon the ftupidity and cowardice of Sophron. The party had not proceeded far, before, by ill fortune, they came to the place where his favourite lamb was feeding; and, as he had not yet learned to dread the cruelty of the human fpecies, he advanced towards them with all the confidence of unfufpicious innocence. This is a lucky accident, cried one of the foldiers, with a brutal fatisfaction; fortune was not willing that we fhould go without a fupper, and has therefore fent us a prefent. A happy exchange, anfwered a fecond; a fat fheep inftead of a lubberly fhepherd; and the coward will no doubt think himfelf happy to fleep in a whole fkin at fo fmall an expence. Saying this, he took the lamb, and bore it away in triumph; uttering a thoufand threats and execrations againft the mafter, if he fhould dare to reclaim it. Sophron was not fo far removed as to efcape

the

the fight of the indignity which was offered him. He followed the troop with so much swiftness, that it was not long before he overtook the soldier who was bearing away his friend, and, from his load, marched rather behind the rest. When Sophron approached him, he accosted him in the gentlest manner, and besought him, in words that might have touched any one but a savage, to restore his favourite. He even offered, when he found nothing else would avail, to purchase back his own property with something of greater value. But the barbarous soldier, inured to scenes of misery, and little accustomed to yield to human entreaties, only laughed at his complaints, and loaded him with additional insults. At length, he began to be tired with his importunities, and, drawing his sword, and waving it before the eyes of Sophron, threatened that, if he did not depart immediately, he would use him as he intended to do the lamb. And do you think, answered Sophron, that, while I have an arm to lift, or a drop of blood in my veins, I will suffer you, or any man, to rob me of what I value more than life? The soldier, exasperated at such an insolent reply, as he termed it, aimed a blow at Sophron with his sword, which

which he turned aside with a stick he held in his hand, so that it glanced inoffensively down; and before he could recover the use of his weapon, Sophron, who was infinitely stronger, closed in with him, wrested it out of his hands, and hurled him roughly to the ground. Some of the comrades of the vanquished soldier came in an instant to his assistance, and, without inquiring into the merits of the cause, drew their swords, and began to assail the undaunted young man. But he, brandishing the weapon which he had just seized, appeared ready to defend himself with so much strength and courage, that they did not choose to come too near. While they were thus engaged, the officer, who had turned back at the first noise of the affray, approached, and, ordering his men to desist, enquired into the occasion of the contest. Sophron then recounted with so much modesty and respect, the indignities and insults he had received, and the unprovoked attack of the soldier, which had obliged him to defend his own life, that the officer, who had a real respect for courage, was charmed with the behaviour of the young man. He therefore reproved his men for their disorderly manners, praised the intrepidity of Sophron, and ordered his

lamb

lamb to be restored to him, with which he joyfully departed.

Sophron was scarcely out of sight, when Tigranes, who was then by accident returning from the chace, met the same party upon their march. Their military attire and glittering arms instantly struck his mind with admiration. He stopped to gaze upon them as they passed, and the officer, who remarked the martial air and well-proportioned limbs of Tigranes, entered into conversation with him, and made him the same proposals which he had before done to Sophron. Such incentives were irresistible to a vain and ambitious mind: the young man in an instant forgot his friends, his country, and his parents, and marched away with all the pleasure that strong presumption and aspiring hopes could raise. Nor was it long before he had an opportunity of signalizing his intrepidity. Asia was at that time overran by numerous bands of savage warriors under different and independent chiefs. That country, which has in every age been celebrated for the mildness of the climate and the fertility of the soil, seems to be destined to groan under all the horrors of eternal servitude. Whether these effects are merely produced by fortune, or whether the
natural

natural advantages it enjoys have a neceſſary tendency to ſoften the minds of the inhabitants to ſloth and effeminacy, it is certain that the people of Aſia have in general been the unreſiſting prey of every invader. At this time, ſeveral fierce and barbarous nations had broken in upon its territory; and, after covering its fertile plains with carnage and deſolation, were contending with each other for the ſuperiority.

Under the moſt enterprizing of theſe rival chiefs was Tigranes now enrolled, and in the very firſt engagement at which he was preſent, he gave ſuch uncommon proofs of valour, that he was diſtinguiſhed by the general with marks of particular regard, and became the admiration of all his comrades. Under the banners of this adventurous warrior did Tigranes toil with various fortunes, during the ſpace of many years. Sometimes victorious in the fight, ſometimes baffled; at one time crowned with conqueſt and glory, at another beſet with dangers, covered with wounds, and hunted like a wild beaſt through rocks and foreſts. Yet ſtill the native courage of his temper ſuſtained his ſpirits and kept him firm in the profeſſion which he had choſen. At length, in a deciſive battle in which the chieftain under whom

whom Tigranes had enlisted contended with the most powerful of his rivals, he had the honour of retrieving the victory, when his own party seemed totally routed; and, after having penetrated the thickest squadrons of the enemy, to kill their general with his own hand. From this moment he seemed to be in possession of all that his ambition could desire. He was appointed general of all the troops, under the chief himself, whose repeated victories had rendered him equal in power to the most celebrated monarchs. Nor did his fortune stop even here; for after a number of successive battles, in which his party were generally victorious by his experience and intrepidity, he was upon the unexpected death of the chief, unanimously chosen by the whole nation to succeed him.

In the mean time Sophron, free from envy, avarice, or ambition, pursued the natural impulse of his character, and contented himself with a life of virtuous obscurity. He pass'd his time in rural labours, in watching his flocks, and in attending with all the duty of an affectionate child upon his aged parents. Every morning he rose with the sun, and spreading his innocent arms to Heaven, thanked that Being which has

created

created all nature, for the continuance of life and health, and all the bleffings he enjoyed. His piety and virtue were rewarded with every thing which a temperate and rational mind can afk. All his rural labours fucceeded in the ampleft manner; his flocks were the faireft, the moft healthy and numerous of the diftrict; he was loved and efteemed by the youth of the neighbourhood, and equally refpected by the aged, who pointed him out as the example of every virtue to their families. But what was more dear than all the reft to fuch a mind as Sophron's, was to fee himfelf the joy, the comfort, and fupport of his parents, who frequently embraced him with tears, and fupplicated the Deity to reward fuch duty and affection with all his choiceft bleffings.

Nor was his humanity confined to his own fpecies; the innocent inhabitants of the foreft were fafe from the purfuit of Sophron, and all that lived under his protection were fure to meet with diftinguifhed tendernefs. It is enough, faid Sophron, that the innocent fheep fupplies me with his fleece, to form my proper garments, and defend me from the cold; I will not bereave him of his little life, nor to ftop his harmlefs gambols on the green, to gratify a guilty fenfuality. It is is surely enough that the stately heifer affords me copious streams of pure and wholesome food; I will not arm my hand against her innocent existence; I will not pollute myself with her blood, nor tear her warm and panting flesh with a cruelty that we abhor even in savage beasts. More wholesome, more adapted to human life are the spontaneous fruits which liberal nature produces for the sustenance of man, or which the earth affords to recompense his labours.

Here the interest and concern which had been long visible in Tommy's face could no longer be represt, and tears began to trickle down his cheeks. What is the matter, my darling, said his mother, what is there in the account of this young man that so deeply interests and affects you?—Alas! said Tommy, mamma, it reminds me of poor Harry Sandford; just such another good young man will he be, when he is as old as Sophron; and I, and I, added he sobbing, am just such another worthless, ungrateful wretch as Tigranes. But Tigranes, said Mrs. Merton, you see, became a great and powerful man, while Sophron remained only a poor and ignorant shepherd. What does that signify, mamma? said Tommy. For my part,

part, I begin to find that it is not always the greateſt people that are the beſt or happieſt; and as to ignorance, I cannot think that Sophron, who underſtood his duty ſo well to his parents, and to God, and to all the world, could be called ignorant, and very likely he could read and write better than Tigranes, in ſpite of all his pomp and grandeur; for I am ſure there is not one of the young gentlemen that went home to-day, that reads as well as Harry Sandford, or has half his underſtanding. Mr. Merton could hardly help ſmiling at Tommy's conjecture about Sophron's reading, but he felt the greateſt pleaſure at ſeeing ſuch a change in his ſentiments; and looking at him with more cordiality than he had done before, he told him that he was very happy to find him ſo ſenſible of his faults, and hoped he would be equally ready to amend them. Miſs Simmons then continued her narrative:

If Sophron ever permitted himſelf to ſhed the blood of living creatures, it was of thoſe ferocious animals that wage continual war with every other ſpecies. Amid the mountains which he inhabited, there were rugged cliffs and inacceſſible caverns, which afforded retreat to wolves, and bears, and tygers. Sometimes, amid the ſtorms and ſnows

snows of winter, they felt themselves pinched by hunger, and fell with almost irresistible fury upon the nearest flocks and herds. Not only sheep and oxen were slaughtered in these dreadful and unexpected attacks, but even the shepherds themselves were frequently the victims of their rage. If there was time to assemble for their defence, the boldest of the youth would frequently seize their arms, and give battle to the invaders. In this warfare, which was equally just and honourable, Sophron was always foremost; his unequalled strength and courage made all the youth adopt him as their leader, and march with confidence under his command. And so succefsful were his expeditions that he always returned loaded with the skins of vanquished enemies, and, by his vigilance and intrepidity, at length either killed or drove away most of the beasts from whom any danger was to be feared.

It happened one day that Sophron had been following the chace of a wolf which had made some depredations upon the flocks, and, in the ardour of his pursuit, was separated from all his companions. He was too well acquainted with the roughest parts of the neighbouring mountains, and too indifferent to danger, to be disturbed at this

this circumstance; he, therefore, followed his flying foe with so much impetuosity, that he completely lost every track and mark with which he was acquainted. As it is difficult, in a wild and uncultivated district, to find the path again, when once it is lost, Sophron only wandered the farther from his home the more he endeavoured to return. He found himself bewildered and entangled in a dreary wilderness, where he was every instant stopped by torrents that tumbled from the neighbouring cliffs, or in danger of slipping down precipices of an immense height. He was alone, in the midst of a gloomy forest where human industry had never penetrated, nor the woodman's ax been heard, since the moment of its creation; to add to his distress, the setting sun disappeared in the west, and the shades of night gathered gradually round, accompanied with the roar of savage beasts: Sophron found himself beset with terrors, but his soul was incapable of fear; he poized his javelin in his hand, and forced his way through every opposition, till at length, with infinite difficulty, he disengaged himself from the forest, just as the last glimmer of light was yet visible in the skies. But it was in vain that he had thus escaped; he cast

cast his eyes around, but could discern nothing but an immense track of country, rough with rocks, and overhung with forests; but destitute of every mark of cultivation or inhabitants. He, however, pursued his way along the side of the mountain, till he descended into a pleasant valley, free from trees and watered by a winding stream. Here he was going to repose for the remainder of the night, under the crag of an impending rock, when a rising gleam of light darted suddenly into the skies from a considerable distance, and attracted his curiosity. Sophron looked towards the quarter whence it came, and plainly discerned that it was a fire, kindled either by some benighted traveller like himself, or by some less innocent wanderers of the dark. He determined to approach the light, but knowing the unsettled state of all the neighbouring districts, he thought it prudent to advance with caution. He therefore made a considerable circuit, and by clambering along the higher grounds, discovered an hanging wood, under whose thick covert he approached without being discovered, within a little distance of the fire. He then preceived that a party of soldiers were reposing round a flaming pile of wood, and

carous-

carousing at their ease; all about was strewn the plunder which they had accumulated in their march, and in the midst was seated a venerable old man, accompanied by a beautiful young woman. Sophron easily comprehended, by the dejection of their countenances, and the tears which trickled down the maiden's cheeks, as well as by the insolence with which they were treated, that they were prisoners. The virtuous indignation of his temper was instantly excited, and he determined to attempt their deliverance. But this, in spite of all his intrepidity, he perceived was no easy matter to accomplish. He was alone and weakly armed; his enemies, though not numerous, too many for him to flatter himself with any rational hope of success by open force; and should he make a fruitless effort, he might rashly throw his life away, and only aggravate the distresses he sought to cure. With this consideration he restrained his natural impetuosity, and at length, determined to attempt by stratagem, what he thought could scarcely be performed by force. He therefore silently withdrew, and skirted the side of the wood which had concealed him, carefully remarking every circumstance of the way, till he had ascended a mouna mountain, which immediately fronted the camp of the foldiers, at no confiderable diftance. He happened to have by his fide a kind of battle-axe which they ufe in the chafe of bears; with this he applied himfelf to lopping the branches of trees, collecting at the fame time all the fallen ones he could find, till, in a fhort time, he had reared feveral piles of wood upon the moft confpicuous part of the mountain, and full in the view of the foldiers. He then eafily kindled a blaze by rubbing two decayed branches together, and in an inftant all the piles were blazing with fo many ftreams of light, that the neighbouring hills and forefts were illuminated with the gleam. Sophron knew the nature of man, always prone to fudden impreffions of fear and terror, more particularly amid the obfcurity of the night, and promifed himfelf the ampleft fuccefs from his ftratagem. In the mean time he haftened back with all the fpeed he could ufe, till he reached the very wood where he had lurked before; he then raifed his voice, which was naturally loud and clear, and fhouted feveral times fucceffively with all his exertion. An hundred echoes from the neighbouring cliffs and caverns returned the found, with a reverberation that made it appear like the noife noise of a mighty squadron. The soldiers, who had been alarmed by the sudden blaze of so many fires, which they attributed to a numerous band of troops, were now impreſt with such a panic that they fled in confusion. They imagined themselves surrounded by their enemies, who were burſting in on every side; and fled with so much precipitation that they were diſperſed in an inſtant, and left the priſoners to themſelves. Sophron, who saw from a small diſtance all their motions, did not wait for them to be undeceived, but running to the spot they had abandoned, explained in a few words to the trembling and amazed captives, the nature of his stratagem, and exhorted them to fly with all the swiftness they were able to exert. Few intreaties were neceſſary to prevail upon them to comply; they therefore arose and followed Sophron, who led them a conſiderable way up into the mountains, and when he thought them out of the immediate danger of purſuit, they sheltered themselves in a rocky cavern, and determined there to wait for the light of the morning.

When they were thus in a place of ſafety, the venerable old man ſeized the hand of Sophron, and, bedewing it with his tears, gave way to the ſtrong emotions of gratitude,

which

which overwhelmed his mind. Generous youth, said he, I know not by what extraordinary fortune you have thus been able to effect our deliverance, when we imagined ourselves out of the reach of human succour; but, if the uniform gratitude and affection of two human beings, who perhaps are not entirely unworthy your regard, can be any recompence for such a distinguished act of virtue, you may command our lives, and employ them in your service.

Father, answered Sophron, you infinitely over-rate the merits of the service which chance has enabled me to perform. I am but little acquainted with my fellow-creatures, as having always inhabited these mountains; but I cannot conceive that any other man who had been witness to your distress would have refused to attempt your rescue. And, as to all the rest, the obscurity of the night, and peculiarity of the situation, rendered it a work of little difficulty or danger. Sophron then recounted to his new friends the accident which had brought him to that unfrequented spot, and made him an unperceived witness of their captivity; he also explained the nature of the stratagem, by which, alone and unsupported, he had been enabled to disperse their enemies,

enemies. He added, that, if he appeared to have any little merit in their eyes, he should be amply recompenfed by being admitted to their friendship and confidence. With thefe mutual profeffions of efteem they thought it prudent to terminate a converfation, which, however agreeable, was not entirely free from danger, as fome of their late oppreffors might happen to diftinguifh their voices, and, thus directed to their lurking-place, exact a fevere revenge for the terrors they had undergone.

With the firft ray of morning the three companions arofe, and Sophron, leading them along the fkirts of the mountains where brufhes and brufh-wood concealed them from obfervation, and ftill following the windings of the river as a guide, they at length came to a cultivated fpot, though deferted by its inhabitants from the fear of the party they had lately efcaped. Here they made a flight and hafty repaft upon fome coarfe provifions which they found, and inftantly ftruck again into the woods, which they judged fafer than the plain. But Sophron fortunately recollected that he had formerly vifited this village with his father, while yet a child, and before the country had fuffered the rage of barbarous
in-

invasions. It was a long day's march from home, but, by exerting all their force, they at length arrived, through rough and secret paths, at the hospitable cottage where Sophron and his parents dwelt. Here they were joyfully received, as the long absence of the young man had much alarmed his parents, and made all the hamlet anxious concerning his safety. That night they comfortably reposed in a place of safety, and the next morning, after a plentiful but coarse repast, the father of Sophron again congratulated his guests upon their fortunate escape, and entreated them to let him hear the history of their misfortunes.

I can refuse nothing, said the venerable stranger, to persons to whom I am under such extraordinary obligations, although the history of my life is short and simple, and contains little worthy to be recited. My name is Chares, and I was born in one of the maritime cities of Asia, of opulent parents, who died while I was yet a youth. The loss of my parents, to whom I was most affectionately attached, made so strong an impression upon my mind, that I determined to seek relief in travel, and, for that purpose, sold my paternal estate, the price of which I converted into money and jewels,

jewels, as being moſt portable. My father had been a man diſtinguiſhed for his knowledge and abilities, and from him I imbibed an early deſire of improvement, which has always been my greateſt comfort and ſupport. The firſt place, therefore, which I viſited was Ægypt, a country renowned in every age for its invention of all the arts which contribute to ſupport or adorn human life. There I reſided ſeveral years, giving up my time to the ſtudy of philoſophy, and to the converſation of the many eminent men who reſorted thither from all the regions of the world. This country is one immenſe plain, divided by the Nile, which is one of the nobleſt rivers in the world, and pours its tide along the middle of its territory. Every year, at a particular ſeaſon, the ſtream begins gradually to ſwell, with ſuch an increaſe of waters, that at length it riſes over its banks, and the whole extent of Ægypt becomes an immenſe lake, where buildings, temples, and cities, appear as floating upon the inundation. Nor is this event a ſubject of dread to the inhabitants: on the contrary, the overflowing of their river is a day of public rejoicing to all the natives, which they celebrate with ſongs and dances, and every ſymptom of extravagant joy. Nor is
this

this to be wondered at, when you are informed that this inundation renders the foil it covers the moſt abundant in the world. Whatever land is covered by the waters receives fuch an increaſe of fertility as never to difappoint the hopes of the induſtrious huſbandman. The inſtant the waters have retired, the farmer returns to his fields and begins the operations of agriculture. Theſe labours are not very difficult in a foft and yielding flime, fuch as the river leaves behind it. The feeds are fown and vegetate with inconceivable rapidity; and, in a few weeks, an abundant harveſt of every kind of grain covers the land. For this reafon, all the neceſſaries of life are eafily procured by the innumerable multitudes which inhabit the country. Nor is the climate lefs favourable than the foil; for here an eternal fpring and fummer feem to have fixed their abode. No froſt, or fnow, is ever known to chill the atmofphere, which is always perfumed with the fmell of aromatic plants that grow on every fide, and bring on a pleafing forgetfulnefs of human care. But, alas! thefe bleffings, great as they may appear, produce the effect of curfes upon the inhabitants. The eafe and plenty which they enjoy enervate their manners, and deftroy

all vigour both of body and mind. No one
is here enflamed with the facred love of his
country, or of public liberty; no one is
inured to arms, or taught to prefer his honour to his life. The great bufinefs of exiftence is an inglorious indolence; a lethargy of mind, and a continual fufpence
from all exertion. The very children catch
the contagion from their parents; they are
inftructed in every effeminate art: to dance
in foft, unmanly attitudes, to modulate their
voice by mufical inftruments, and to adjuft
the floating drapery of their drefs, thefe are
the arts in which both fexes are inftructed
from their infancy. But no one is taught
to wield the arms of men, to tame the noble
fteeds in which the country abounds, to obferve his rank in war, or to bear the in-
difpenfable hardfhips of a military life.
Hence this celebrated country, which has
been in every age the admiration of mankind, is deftined to the moft degrading
fervitude. A few thoufand difciplined troops
are fufficient to hold the many millions it
contains in bondage, under which they
groan, without ever conceiving the defign
of vindicating their natural rights by arms.—
Unhappy people! exclaimed Sophron, how
ufelefs to them are all the bleffings of their
climate!

climate! How much rather would I inhabit the stormy top of Lebanon, amid eternal snows and barrenness, than wallow in the vile sensuality of such a country, or breathe an air infected by its vices!

Chares was charmed with the generous indignation of Sophron, and thus continued:—I was of the same opinion with yourself, and therefore determined to leave a country which all its natural advantages could not render agreeable, when I understood the manners of its inhabitants. But, before I quitted that part of the globe, my curiosity led me to visit the neighbouring tribes of Arabia, a nation bordering upon the Ægyptians, but as different in spirits and manners as the hardy shepherds of these mountains from the effeminate natives of the plains. Ægypt is bounded on one side by the sea; on every other, it is surrounded by immense plains or gentle eminences, which being beyond the reach of the fertilizing inundations of the Nile, have been, beyond all memory, converted into waste and barren sands by the excessive heat of the sun. I, therefore, made preparations for my journey, and hired a guide, who was to furnish me with beasts of burthen, and accompany me across those dreary deserts.

ferts. We accordingly began our march, mounted each upon a camel, which are found much more ufeful than horfes in fuch a burning climate.

Indeed, faid Tommy here to Mr. Barlow, I am forry to interrupt the ftory, but I fhall be much obliged to you, fir, if you will inform me what kind of an animal a camel is.

The camel, anfwered Mr. Barlow, is chiefly found in thofe burning climates which you have heard defcribed. His height is very great, rifing to fourteen or fifteen feet, reckoning to the top of his head. His legs are long and flender, his body not large, and his neck of an amazing length. This animal is found, in no part of the world that we are acquainted with, wild or free, but the whole race is enflaved by man, and brought up to drudgery from the firft moment of their exiftence. As foon as he is born, they feize him and force him to recline upon the ground, with his legs doubled up under his belly. To keep him in this attitude they extend a piece of canvas over his body, and fix it to the ground by laying heavy weights upon the edge. In this manner he is tutored to obedience, and taught to kneel down at the

orders

orders of his master, and receive the burthens which he is destined to transport. In his temper he is gentle and tractable, and his patience in bearing thirst and hunger is superior to that of any animal we are acquainted with. He is driven across the burning deserts, loaded with the merchandize of those countries, and frequently does not find even water to quench his thirst for several days. As to his food, it is nothing but the few herbs which are found in the least barren parts of the deserts, and prickly bushes, upon which he browzes as a delicacy: sometimes he does not find even these for many days, yet pursues his journey with a degree of patience which is hardly credible.

We mounted our camels, continued Chares, and soon had reached the confines of the fertile plains of Ægypt. The way, as we proceeded, grew sensibly more dreary and disagreeable, yet was sometimes varied with little tufts of trees and scanty patches of herbage. But these at length entirely disappeared, and nothing was seen on every side but an immense extent of barren sands, destitute of vegetation, and parched by the continual heat of the sun. No sound was heard to interrupt the dreary silence that reigned around, no traces of inhabitants perceivable, and the gloomy uniformity of the prospect inspired the soul with melancholy. In the mean time, the sun seemed to shoot down perpendicular rays upon our heads, without a cloud to mitigate his violence. I felt a burning fever take possession of my body; my tongue was scorched with intolerable heat, and it was in vain I endeavoured to moisten my mouth with repeated draughts of water. At night we came to a little rising ground, at the foot of which we perceived some aquatic herbs and a small quantity of muddy water, of which our camels took prodigious draughts. Here we spread our tents and encamped for the night. With the morning we pursued our journey, but had not proceeded far, before we saw a cloud of dust that seemed to rise along the desert; and, as we approached nearer, we easily distinguished the glitter of arms that reflected the rising sun. This was a band of the Arabians that had discovered us and came to know our intentions. As they advanced, they spurred their horses, which are the most fleet and excellent in the world, and bounded along the desert with the lightness of an antelope; at the same time they brandished their lances, and seemed prepared alike for war or peace. But

But when they saw that we had neither the intention, nor the power to commit hostilities, they stopped their coursers at the distance of a few paces from us; and he, that appeared the chief, advanced, and, with a firm but mild tone of voice, enquired into the reason of our coming. It was then that I took the liberty of addressing him in his own language, to which I had for some time applied myself before my journey. I explained to him the curiosity which led me to observe in person the manners of a people, who are celebrated over the whole world, for having preserved their native simplicity unaltered and their liberty unviolated, amid the revolutions which agitate all the neighbouring nations. I then offered to him the loading of my camel, which I had brought not as being worthy his acceptance, but as a slight testimony of my regard; and concluded with remarking, that the fidelity of the Arabians in observing their engagements was unimpeached in a single instance; and therefore, relying upon the integrity of my own intentions, I had come a painful journey, unarmed, and almost alone, to put myself into their power, and demand the sacred rights of hospitality.

While

While I was thus speaking, he looked at me with a penetration that seemed to read into my very soul; and when I had finished, he extended his arm with a smile of benevolence, and welcomed me to their tribe; telling me at the same time, that they admitted me as their guest and received me with the arms of friendship: that their method of life, like their manners, was coarse and simple, but that I might consider myself as safer in their tents, and more removed from violence or treachery, than in the crowded cities which I had left. The rest of the squadron then approached, and all saluted me as a friend and brother. We then struck off across the desert, and after a few hours march approached the encampment where they had left their wives and children.

This people is the most singular, and in many respects the most admirable of all that inhabit this globe of earth. All other nations are subject to revolutions and the various turns of fortune. Sometimes they wage successful wars; sometimes they improve in the arts of peace; now they are great and reverenced by their neighbours; and now, insulted and despised, they suffer all the miseries of servitude. The Arabians

bians alone have never been known to vary in the smallest circumstance either of their internal policy or external situation. They inhabit a climate which would be intolerable to the rest of the human species for its burning heat, and a soil which refuses to furnish any of the necessaries of life. Hence, they neither plough the earth, nor sow, nor depend upon corn, for their sustenance, nor are acquainted with any of the mechanic arts. They live chiefly upon the milk of their herds and flocks, and sometimes eat their flesh. These burning deserts are stretched out to an immense extent on every side, and these they consider as their common country, without having any fixed or permanent place of abode. Arid and barren as are these wilds in general, there are various spots which are more productive than the rest. Here are found supplies of water and some appearances of vegetation; and here the Arabians encamp till they have exhausted the spontaneous products of the soil. Besides, they vary their place of residence with the different seasons of the year. When they are in perfect friendship with their neighbours, they advance to the very edges of the desert, and find more ample supplies of moisture and herbage. If they

they are attacked or molested, the whole tribe is in motion in an instant, and seeks a refuge in their impenetrable recesses. Other nations are involved in various pursuits of war, or government, or commerce; they have made a thousand inventions of luxury necessary to their welfare, and the enjoyment of these they call happiness. The Arab is ignorant of all these things, or, if he knows them, despises their possession. All his wants, his passions, his desires, terminate in one object, and that object is the preservation of his liberty. For this purpose he contents himself with a bare sufficiency of the coarsest and simplest food; and the small quantity of cloathing which he requires in such a climate is fabricated by the women of the tribe, who milk the cattle and prepare the food of their husbands, and require no other pleasures than the pleasing interest of domestic cares. They have a breed of horses superior to any in the rest of the globe for gentleness, patience, and unrivalled swiftness. This is the particular passion and pride of the Arabian tribes. They are necessary to them in their warlike expeditions and in their courses along the deserts. If they are attacked, they mount their steeds, who bear them with the rapidity of a tempest, to avenge their injuries;

ries; or should they be overmatched in fight, they soon transport them beyond the possibility of pursuit. For this reason the proudest monarchs and greatest conquerors have in vain endeavoured to subdue them. Troops accustomed to the plenty of a cultivated country are little able to pursue these winged warriors, over the wide extent of their sandy wastes. Opprest with heat, fainting for want of water, and spent with the various difficulties of the way, the most numerous armies have been destroyed in such attempts; and those that survived the obstacles of nature, were easily overcome by the repeated attacks of the valiant natives.

While I was in this country, I was myself witness to an embassy that was sent from a neighbouring prince, who imagined the fame of his exploits had struck the Arabians with terror, and disposed them to submission. The ambassador was introduced to the chief of the tribe, a venerable old man, undistinguished by any mark of ostentation from the rest, who received him sitting crofs-legged at the door of his tent. He then began to speak, and in a long and studied harangue, described the power of his master, the invincible courage of his armies, the vast profusion of arms, of warlike engines, and military stores, and

con-

concluded with a demand that the Arabians should submit to acknowledge him as their lord and pay a yearly tribute. At this proud speech, the younger part of the tribe began to frown with indignation and clash their weapons in token of defiance; but the chief himself, with a calm and manly composure, made this reply: I expected from the maturity of your age, and the gravity of your countenance, to have heard a rational discourse, befitting you to propose and us to hear. When you dwelt so long upon the power of your master, I also imagined that he had sent to us to propose a league of friendship and alliance, such as might become equals, and bind man more closely to his fellows. In this case the Arabians, although they neither want the assistance, nor fear the attacks of any king or nation, would gladly have consented; because it has been always their favourite maxim neither to leave injuries unpunished, nor to be outdone in kindness and hospitality. But since you have come thus far to deliver a message, which must needs be disagreeable to the ears of free-born men, who acknowledge no superior upon earth, you may thus report the sentiments of the Arabians to him that sent you.

You

You may tell him, that as to the land which we inhabit, it is neither the gift of him nor any of his fore-fathers; we hold it from our anceſtors, who received it in turn for theirs, by the common laws of nature, which has adapted particular countries and ſoils not only to man, but to all the various animals which ſhe has produced. If, therefore, your king imagines that he has a right to retain the country which he and his people now inhabit, by the ſame tenure do the Arabians hold the ſovereignty of theſe barren ſands; where the bones of their anceſtors have been buried, even from the firſt creation of the world. But you have deſcribed to us in pompous language, the extraordinary power and riches of your king; according to you, he not only commands numerous and well-appointed troops of warlike men, furniſhed with every ſpecies of military ſtores, but he alſo poſſeſſes immenſe heaps of gold, ſilver, and other precious commodities, and his country affords him an inexhauſtible ſupply of corn and oil and wine, and all the other conveniencies of life. If, therefore, this repreſentation be falſe, you muſt appear a vain and deſpicable babbler, who, being induced by no ſufficient reaſon, have come hither

of

of your own accord to amuſe us, a plain and ſimple race of men, with ſpecious tales and fables; but, if your words be true, your king muſt be equally unjuſt and fooliſh, who, already poſſeſſed of all theſe advantages, doth ſtill inſatiably graſp after more; and enjoying ſo many good things with eaſe and ſecurity to himſelf, will rather put them all to the hazard, than repreſs the vain deſires of his own intolerable avarice. As to the tribute which you have demanded, what you have already ſeen of the Arabians and their country may afford you a ſufficient anſwer. You ſee that we have neither cities, nor fields, nor rivers, nor wine, nor oil; gold and ſilver are equally unknown among us; and the Arabians, abandoning all theſe things to other men, have, at the ſame time delivered themſelves from the neceſſity of being ſlaves, which is the general law by which all other mortals retain their poſſeſſions. We have, therefore, nothing which we can ſend as a tribute but the ſands of theſe our deſerts, and the arrows and lances with which we have hitherto defended them from all invaders. If theſe are treaſures worthy of his acceptance, he may lead his conquering troops to take poſſeſſion of our country.

But

But he will find men who are not softened by luxury, or vanquished by their own vices; men, who prize their liberty at a dearer rate than all other mortals do their riches or their lives; and to whom dishonour is more formidable than wounds and death. If he can vanquish such men, it will, however, become his prudence to reflect, whether he can vanquish the obstacles which nature herself has opposed to his ambition. In attempting to pass our deserts, he will have to struggle with famine and consuming thirst; from which no enemy has hitherto escaped, even when he has failed to perish by the arrows of the Arabians.

Happy and generous people, exclaimed Sophron, how well do they deserve the liberty they enjoy! With such sentiments they need not fear the attack of kings or conquerors. It is the vices of men, and not the weakness of their nature, that basely enslave them to their equals; and he that prizes liberty beyond a few contemptible pleasures of his senses, may be certain that no human force can ever bereave him of so great a good.

Such sentiments, replied Chares, convince me that I have not made a false es-
timate

timate of the inhabitants of these mountainous districts. It is for this reason that I have been so particular in the description of Ægypt and Arabia. I wished to know whether the general spirit of indolence and pusillanimity had infected the hardy inhabitants of Lebanon: but from the generous enthusiasm which animates your countenance at the recital of noble actions, as well as from what I have experienced, you are capable of attempting, I trust that these solitary scenes are uninfected with the vices that have deluged the rest of Asia, and bent its inhabitants to the yoke.

Here the impatience of Tommy, which had been encreasing a considerable time, could no longer be restrained, and he could not help interrupting the story, by addressing Mr. Barlow thus:

Tommy.

Sir, you will give me leave to ask you a question?

Mr. Barlow.

As many as you choose.

Tommy.

In all these stories which I have heard, it

it seems as if those nations, that have little or nothing, are more good-natured, and better, and braver, than those that have a great deal.

Mr. BARLOW.

This is indeed sometimes the case.

TOMMY.

But then, why should it not be the case here, as well as in other places? Are all the poor in this country better than the rich?

It should seem, answered Mr. Barlow smiling, as you were of that opinion.

TOMMY.

Why so, sir?

Mr. BARLOW.

Because, whatever you want to have done, I observe that you always address yourself to the poor, and not to the rich.

TOMMY.

Yes, sir, but that is a different case. The poor are used to do many things which the rich never do.

Mr. BARLOW.

Are those things useful, or not useful?

TOMMY.

Tommy.

Why, to be sure, many of them are extremely useful; for, since I have acquired so much knowledge, I find they cultivate the ground to raise corn, aud build houses, and hammer iron, which is so necessary to make every thing we use; besides feeding cattle, and dressing our victuals, and washing our cloaths, and, in short, doing every thing which is necessary to be done.

Mr. Barlow.

What, do the poor do all these things?

Tommy.

Yes, indeed, or else they never would be done. For it would be a very ungenteel thing to labour at a forge like a blacksmith, or hold the plough like a farmer, or build an house like a bricklayer.

Mr. Barlow.

And did not you build an house in my garden some little time ago?

Tommy.

Yes, sir, but that was only for my amusement. It was not intended for any body to live in.

Mr. BARLOW.

So you still think it the first qualification of a gentleman never to do any thing useful; and he that does any thing with that design ceases to be a gentleman.

Tommy looked a little ashamed at this, but he said it was not so much his own opinion, as that of the other young gentlemen and ladies with whom he had conversed.

But, replied Mr. Barlow, you asked just now which were the best, the rich or the poor; but if the poor provide food, and cloathing, and houses, and every thing else, not only for themselves but for all the rich, while the rich do nothing at all, it must appear that the poor are better than the rich.

TOMMY.

Yes, sir, but then the poor do not act in that manner out of kindness, but because they are obliged to it.

Mr. BARLOW.

That indeed is a better argument than you sometimes use. But tell me which set of people would you prefer, those that are always doing useful things because they are

VOL. III. D obliged

obliged to it, or those who never do any thing useful at all?

TOMMY.

Indeed, sir, I hardly know what to say, but when I asked the question, I did not so much mean the doing useful things.—But now I think on it, the rich do a great deal of good by buying the things of the poor, and giving them money in return.

Mr. BARLOW.

What is money?

TOMMY.

Money, sir, money is———I believe little pieces of silver and gold, with an head upon them.

Mr. BARLOW.

And what is the use of these little pieces of silver and gold?

TOMMY.

Indeed I do not know that they are of any use. But every body has agreed to take them, and therefore you may buy with them whatever you want.

Mr.

Mr. BARLOW.

Then, according to your laſt account, the goodneſs of the rich confiſts in taking from the poor houſes, cloaths, and food, and giving them in return little bits of ſilver and gold, which are really good for nothing.

TOMMY.

Yes, ſir; but then the poor can take theſe pieces of money and purchaſe every thing which they want.

Mr. BARLOW.

You mean, that, if a poor man has money in his pocket, he can always exchange it for cloaths, or food, or any other neceſſary.

TOMMY.

Indeed I do, ſir.

Mr. BARLOW.

But who muſt he buy them of?—For, according to your account, the rich never produce any of theſe things; therefore, the poor, if they want to purchaſe them, can only do it of each other.

TOMMY.

But, sir, I cannot think that is always the case; for, I have been along with my mamma to shops, where there were fine powdered gentlemen and ladies that sold things to other people, and livery servants, and young ladies that played upon the harpsichord like Miss Matilda.

Mr. BARLOW.

But, my good little friend, do you imagine that these fine powdered gentlemen and ladies made the things which they sold?

TOMMY.

That, sir, I cannot tell, but I should rather imagine not; for all the fine people I have ever seen are too much afraid of spoiling their cloaths to work.

Mr. BARLOW.

All that they do, then, is to employ poorer persons to work for them, while they only sell what is produced by their labour. So that still you see we reach no farther than this; the rich do nothing and produce nothing, and the poor every thing that is really useful. Were there a whole nation of

rich

rich people, they would all be starved like the Spaniard in the story, because no one would condescend to produce any thing: and this would happen in spite of all their money, unless they had neighbours who were poorer to supply them. But a nation that was poor might be industrious, and gradually supply themselves with all they wanted; and then it would be of little consequence whether they had pieces of metal with heads upon them or not.——But this conversation has lasted long enough at present, and, as you are now going to bed, I dare say Miss Simmons will be so good as to defer the remainder of her story until tomorrow.

The next day Tommy rose before his father and mother, and, as his imagination had been forcibly acted on by the description he had heard of the Arabian horsemen, he desired his little horse might be saddled, and that William, his father's man, would attend him upon a ride. Unfortunately for Tommy, his vivacity was greater than his reason, and his taste for imitation was continually leading him into some mischief or misfortune. He had no sooner been introduced into the acquaintance of genteel life, than he threw aside all his former habits, and

and burnt to diſtinguiſh himſelf as a moſt accompliſhed young gentleman. He was now, in turn, ſickened and diſguſted with faſhionable affectation, and his mind, at leiſure for freſh impreſſions, was ready to catch at the firſt new object which occurred. The idea, therefore, which preſented itſelf to his mind, as ſoon as he opened his eyes, was that of being an Arabian horſeman. Nothing, he imagined, could equal the the pleaſure of guiding a fiery ſteed over thoſe immenſe and deſolate waſtes which he had heard deſcribed. In the mean time, as the country where he wiſhed to exhibit was rather at too great a diſtance, he thought he might excite ſome applauſe even upon the common before his father's houſe. Full of this idea, he roſe, put on his boots, and ſummoned William to attend him. William had been too much accuſtomed to humour all his caprices, to make any difficulty of obeying him; and, as he had often ridden out with his young maſter before, he did not foreſee the leaſt poſſible inconvenience. But the maternal care of Mrs. Merton had made it an indiſpenſable condition with her ſon, that he ſhould never preſume to ride with ſpurs, and ſhe had ſtrictly enjoined all the ſervants never to

ſupply

supply him with those dangerous implements. Tommy had long murmured in secret at this prohibition, which seemed to imply a distrust of his abilities in horsemanship, which sensibly wounded his pride. But, since he had taken it into his head to emulate the Arabs themselves, and perhaps excel them in their own art, he considered it as no longer possible to endure the disgrace. But, as he was no stranger to the strict injunction which had been given to all the servants, he did not dare to make the experiment of soliciting their assistance. While he was in this embarrassment, a new and sudden expedient presented itself to his fertile genius, which he instantly resolved to adopt. Tommy went to his mamma's maid, and, without difficulty, obtained from her a couple of the biggest pins, which he thrust through the leather of his boots, and, thus accoutred, he mounted his horse without suspicion or observation. Tommy had not ridden far before he began to give vent to his reigning passion, and asked William if he had ever seen an Arabian on horseback. The answer of William sufficiently proved his ignorance, which Tommy kindly undertook to remove by giving him a detail of all the particulars he had heard the preceding

ceding night. But, unfortunately, the eloquence of Tommy precipitated him into a dangerous experiment; for, juſt as he was deſcribing their rapid flight acroſs the deſerts, the intereſt of his ſubject ſo tranſported him, that he cloſed his legs upon his little horſe, and pricked him in ſo ſenſible a manner, that the poney, who was not deficient in ſpirit, reſented the attack, and ſet off with him at a prodigious rate. William, when he ſaw his maſter thus burſt forth, was at a loſs whether to conſider it as an accident, or only an oratorical grace; but, ſeeing the horſe hurrying along the rougheſt part of the common, while Tommy tugged in vain to reſtrain his efforts, he thought it neceſſary to endeavour to overtake, and therefore purſued him with all the ſpeed he could uſe. But the poney, whoſe blood ſeemed to be only the more enflamed by the violence of his own exertions, ran the faſter when he heard the trampling of another horſe behind him. In this manner did Tommy ſcamper over the common, while William purſued in vain; for, juſt as the ſervant thought he had reached his maſter, his horſe would puſh forward with ſuch rapidity as left his purſuer far behind. Tommy kept his ſeat with infinite addreſs,

but

but he now began ferioufly to repent of his own ungovernable ambition, and would, with the greateft pleafure, have exchanged his own fpirited fteed for the dulleft afs in England. The race had now endured a confiderable time, and feemed to be no nearer to a conclufion, when on a fudden, the poney turned fhort, upon an attempt of his mafter to ftop him, and rufhed precipitately into a large bog, or quagmire, which was full before him; here he made a momentary halt, and Tommy wifely embraced the opportunity of letting himfelf flide off upon a foft and yielding bed of mire. The fervant now came up to Tommy, and refcued him from his difagreeable fituation, where, however, he had received no other damage than that of daubing himfelf all over. William had been at firft very much frightened at the danger of his mafter, but, when he faw that he had fo luckily efcaped all hurt, he could not help afking him, with a fmile, whether this too was a ftroke of Arabian horfemanfhip. Tommy was a little provoked at this reflection upon his horfemanfhip, but, as he had now loft fomething of his irritability by repeated mortification, he wifely repreffed his paffion, and defired William to catch his horse, while he returned homewards on foot to warm himself. The servant, therefore, endeavoured to approach the poney, who, as if contented with the triumph he had obtained over his rider, was quietly feeding at a little distance; but, the instant William approached, he set off again at a violent rate, and seemed disposed to lead him a second chace not inferior to the first.

In the mean time, Tommy walked pensively along the common, reflecting upon the various accidents which had befallen him, and the repeated disappointments he had found in all his attempts to distinguish himself. While he was thus engaged, he overtook a poor and ragged figure, the singularity of whose appearance engaged his attention. It was a man of middle age, in a dress he had never seen before, with two poor children that seemed with difficulty to keep up with him, while he carried a third in his arms, whose pale, emaciated looks, sufficiently declared disease and pain. The man had upon his head a coarse blue bonnet instead of an hat; he was wrapped round by a tattered kind of garment, striped with various colours, and, at his side, hung down a long and formidable sword. Tommy
surveyed

surveyed him with such an earnest observation, that, at length, the man took notice of it, and, bowing to him with the greatest civility, ventured to ask him if he had met with any accident, that he appeared in a disorder which suited so little with his quality. Tommy was not a little pleased with the discernment of the man, that could distinguish his importance in spite of the dirtiness of his cloaths, and therefore mildly answered; No, friend, there is not much the matter.—I have a little obstinate horse that ran away with me, and, after trying in vain to throw me down, he plunged into the middle of that great bog there, and so I jumped off for fear of being swallowed up, otherwise I should soon have made him submit; for I am used to such things, and don't mind them in the least. Here the child that the man was carrying began to cry bitterly, and the father endeavoured to pacify him, but in vain. Poor thing, said Tommy, he seems not to be well—I am heartily sorry for him.—Alas! master answered the man, he is not well, indeed; he has now a violent ague fit upon him, and I have not had a morsel of bread to give him, or any of the rest, since yesterday noon. Tommy was naturally generous, and now his mind was unufually foftened by the remembrance of his own recent diftreffes; he therefore pulled a fhilling out of his pocket and gave it to the man, faying, Here, my honeft friend, here is fomething to buy your child fome food, and I fincerely wifh he may foon recover. God blefs your fweet face! faid the man; you are the beft friend I have feen this many a day; but for this kind affiftance we might have all been loft. He then, with many bows and thanks, ftruck acrofs the common into a different path; and Tommy went forward, feeling a greater pleafure at this little act of humanity than he had long been acquainted with among all the fine acquaintance he had lately contracted. But he had walked a very little way with thefe reflections, before he met with a new adventure; a flock of fheep was running with all the precipitation which fear could infpire from the purfuit of a large dog, and juft as Tommy approached, the dog had overtaken a lamb, and feemed difpofed to devour it. Tommy was naturally an enemy to all cruelty, and therefore running towards the dog, with more alacrity than prudence, he endeavoured to drive him from his prey. But the animal, who probably defpifed the diminutive fize of his adverfary,

adverfary, after growling a little while and fhowing his teeth, when he found that this was not fufficient to deter him from intermeddling, intirely quitted the fheep; and, making a fudden fpring, feized upon the fkirt of Tommy's coat, which he fhook with every expreffion of rage. Tommy behaved with more intrepidity than could have been expected, for he neither cried out nor attempted to run, but made his utmoft efforts to difengage himfelf from his enemy. But as the conteft was fo unequal, it is probable he would have been feverely bitten, had not the honeft ftranger, whom he had relieved, come running up to his affiftance, and feeing the danger of his benefactor, laid the dog dead at his feet by a furious ftroke of his broad-fword. Tommy, thus delivered from the impending danger, expreffed his gratitude to the ftranger in the moft affectionate manner, and defired him to accompany him to his father's houfe; where he and his wearied children fhould receive whatever refrefhment they wifhed. He then turned his eyes to the lamb, which had been the caufe of the conteft, and lay panting upon the ground, bleeding and wounded, but not to death, and remarked, with aftonifhment, upon his fleece, the well-known characters

of

of H. S. accompanied with a crofs! As I live, faid Tommy, I believe this is the very lamb which Harry ufed to be fo fond of, and which ufed fometimes to follow him to Mr. Barlow's. I am the luckieft fellow in the world to have come in time to deliver him; and now, perhaps, Harry may forgive me all the ill ufage he has met with. Saying this, he took the lamb up, and kiffed it with the greateft tendernefs; nay, he would have even borne it home in his arms had it not been rather too heavy for his ftrength: but the honeft ftranger, with a grateful officioufnefs, offered his fervices, and prevailed on Tommy to let him carry it, while he delivered his child to the biggeft of its brothers.

When Tommy was now arrived within a little diftance of his home, he met his father and Mr. Barlow, who had left the houfe to enjoy the morning air before breakfaft. They were furprized to fee him in fuch an equipage; for the dirt, which had befpattered him from head to foot, began to dry in various places, and gave him the appearance of a farmer's clay-built wall in the act of hardening. But Tommy, without giving them time to make inquiries, ran affectionately up to Mr. Barlow, and taking him by the

the hand, said; Oh, sir! here is the luckiest accident in the world—poor Harry Sandford's favourite lamb would have been killed by a great mischievous dog, if I had not happened to come by and save his life. And who is this honest man, said Mr. Merton, whom you have picked up upon the common? He seems to be in distress, and his famished children are scarcely able to drag themselves along. Poor man, answered Tommy, I am very much obliged to him; for, when I went to save Harry's lamb, the dog attacked me and would have hurt me very much, if he had not come to my assistance, and killed him with his great sword. So I have brought him with me that he might refresh himself with his poor children, one of which has a terrible ague. For I knew, papa, though I have not behaved well of late, you would not be against my doing an act of charity. I am, on the contrary, very glad, said Mr. Merton, to see you have so much gratitude in your temper. But what is the reason that I see you thus disfigured with dirt? Surely you must have been riding, and your horse have thrown you. And so it is, for here is William following with both the horses in a foam. William at that moment appeared,

ed, and, trotting up to his mafter, began to make excufes for his own fhare in the bufinefs. Indeed, fir, faid he, I did not think there was the leaft harm in going out with mafter Tommy; and we were riding along as quietly as poffible, and mafter was giving me a long account of the Arabs; who, he faid, lived in the fineft country in the world, which does not produce any thing to eat, or drink, or wear; and yet they never want or come upon the parifh; but ride the moft mettled horfes in the world, fit to ftart for any place in England. And juft as he was giving me this account, Punch took it into his head to run away, and while I was endeavouring to catch him, he jumped into a quagmire, and fhot mafter Tommy off in the middle of it. No, faid Tommy, there you miftake; I believe I could manage a much more fpirited horfe than Punch; but I thought it prudent to throw myfelf off, for fear of his plunging deeper in the mire. But how is this, faid Mr. Merton? The poney ufed to be the quieteft of horfes; what can have given him this fudden impulfe to run away? Sure, William, you were not fo imprudent as to truft your mafter with fpurs. No, fir, anfwered William, not I, and I can take

take my oath he had no spurs on when we set out. Mr. Merton was convinced there was some mystery in this transaction, and looking at his son to find it out, he, at length, discovered the ingenious contrivance of Tommy to supply the place of spurs, and could hardly preserve his gravity at the sight. He, however, mildly set before him his imprudence, which might have been attended with the most fatal consequences, the fracture of his limbs, or even the loss of his life, and desired him for the future to be more cautious. They then returned to the house, and Mr. Merton ordered the servants to supply his guests with plenty of the most nourishing food. After breakfast, they sent for the unhappy stranger into the parlour, whose countenance now bespoke his satisfaction and gratitude; and Mr. Merton, who by his dress and accent discovered him to be an inhabitant of Scotland, desired to know by what accident he had thus wandered so far from home with these poor helpless children, and had been reduced to so much misery. Alas! your honour, answered the man, I should ill deserve the favours you have shewn me, if I attempted to conceal any thing from such worthy benefactors. My tale, however, is
simple

THE HISTORY OF

simple and uninteresting, and I fear there can be nothing in the story of my distress the least deserving of your attention. Surely, said Mr. Merton, with the most benevolent courtesy, there must be something in the distress of every honest man which ought to interest his fellow-creatures: and if you will acquaint us with all the circumstances of your situation, it may perhaps be within our power, as it certainly is in our inclinations, to do you farther service. The man then bowed to the company with an air of dignity which surprized them all, and thus began :—I was born in that part of our island which is called the North of Scotland. The country there, partly from the barrenness of the soil and the inclemency of the seasons, and partly from other causes which I will not now enumerate, is unfavourable to the existence of its inhabitants. More than half the year our mountains are covered with continual snows, which prohibit the use of agriculture, or blast the expectations of an harvest. Yet the race of men which inhabit these dreary wilds, are perhaps not more undeserving the smiles of fortune than many of their happier neighbours. Accustomed to a life of toil and hardship, their bodies

are

are braced by the inceſſant difficulties they have to encounter, and their minds remain untainted by the example of their more luxurious neighbours. They are bred up from infancy with a deference and reſpect for their parents, and with a mutual ſpirit of endearment towards their equals, which I have not remarked in happier climates. Theſe circumſtances expand and elevate the mind, and attach the highlanders to their native mountains with a warmth of affection, which is ſcarcely known in the midſt of poliſhed cities and cultivated countries. Every man there is more or leſs acquainted with the hiſtory of his clan, and the martial exploits which they have performed. In the winter ſeaſon we ſit around the blazing light of our fires, and commemorate the glorious actions of our anceſtors; the children catch the ſound, and conſider themſelves as intereſted in ſupporting the honour of a nation, which is yet unſullied in the annals of the world, and reſolve to tranſmit it equally pure to their poſterity. With theſe impreſſions, which were the earlieſt I can remember, you cannot wonder, gentlemen, that I ſhould early imbibe a ſpirit of enterprize and a love of arms. My father was, indeed, poor, but
he

he had been himself a soldier, and therefore did not so strenuously oppose my growing inclinations. He, indeed, set before me the little chance I should have of promotion, and the innumerable difficulties of my intended profession. But what were difficulties to a youth brought up to subsist upon a handful of oatmeal, to drink the waters of the stream, and to sleep, shrouded in my plaid, beneath the arch of an impending rock! I see, gentlemen, continued the highlander, that you appear surprized to hear a man, who has so little to recommend him, express himself in rather loftier language than you are accustomed to among your peasantry here. But you should remember that a certain degree of education is more general in Scotland than where you live; and that, wanting almost all the gifts of fortune, we cannot afford to suffer those of nature to remain uncultivated. When, therefore, my father saw that the determined bent of my temper was towards a military life, he thought in vain to oppose my inclinations. He even, perhaps, involuntarily cherished them, by explaining to me, during the long leisure of our dreary winter, some books which treated of military sciences and ancient history. From these

these I imbibed an early love of truth and honour, which I hope has not abandoned me since; and, by teaching me what brave and virtuous men have suffered in every age and country, they have, perhaps, prevented me from entirely sinking under my misfortunes.

One night in the autumn of the year, as we were seated round the embers of our fire, we heard a knocking at the door. My father rose, and a man of a majestic presence came in and requested permission to pass the night in our cottage. He told us he was an English officer who had long been stationed in the highlands; but now, upon the breaking out of war, he had been sent for in haste to London, whence he was to embark for America as soon as he could be joined by his regiment. This, said he, has been the reason of my travelling later than prudence permits in a mountainous country with which I am imperfectly acquainted. I have unfortunately lost my way, and, but for your kindness, added he smiling, I must here begin my campaign, and pass the night upon a bed of heath amid the mountains. My father rose and received the officer with all the courtesy he was able; for in Scotland every man thinks

thinks himself honoured by being permitted to exercise his hospitality; he told him his accommodations were mean and poor, but what he had was heartily at his service. He then sent me to look after his visitor's horse, and set before him some milk and oaten bread, which were all the dainties we possessed: our guest, however, seemed to feed upon it with an appetite as keen as if he had been educated in the highlands; and, what I could not help remarking with astonishment, although his air and manners proved that he could be no stranger to a more delicate way of living, not a single word fell from him that intimated he had ever been used to better fare. During the evening he entertained us with various accounts of the dangers he had already escaped, and the service he had seen. He particularly described the manners of the savage tribes he was going to encounter in America, and the nature of their warfare. All this, accompanied with the tone and look of a man that was familiar with great events, and had borne a considerable share in all he related, so enflamed my military ardour, that I was no longer capable of repressing it. The stranger perceived it, and, looking at me with an air of tenderness and

com-

compaffion, afked if that young man was intended for the fervice. My colour rofe, and my heart immediately fwelled at the queftion; the look and manner of our gueft had ftrangely interefted me in his favour, and the natural grace and fimplicity with which he related his own exploits put me in mind of the great men of other times. Could I but march under the banners of fuch a leader, I thought nothing would be too arduous to be atchieved. I faw a long perfpective before me of combats, difficulties, and dangers; fomething, however, whifpered to my mind that I fhould be fuccefsful in the end, and fupport the reputation of our name and clan. Full of thefe ideas, I fprang forwards at the queftion, and told the officer that the darling paffion of my life would be to bear arms under a chief like him; and that, if he would fuffer me to enlift under his command, I fhould be ready to juftify his kindnefs by patiently fupporting every hardfhip, and facing every danger. Young man, replied he, with a look of kind concern, there is not an officer in the army that would not be proud of fuch a recruit; but I fhould ill repay the hofpitality I have received from your parents, if I fuffered you to be deceived

ceived in your opinion of the military profession. He then set before me, in the strongest language, all the hardships which would be my lot; the dangers of the field, the pestilence of camps, the slow consuming languor of hospitals, the insolence of command, the mortification of subordination, and the uncertainty that the exertions of even a long life would ever lead to the least promotion. All this, replied I, trembling with fear that my father should take advantage of these too just representations to refuse his consent, I knew before; but I feel an irresistible impulse within me which compels me to the field. The die is cast for life or death, and I will abide by the chance that now occurs. If you, sir, refuse me, I will however enlist with the first officer that will accept me; for I will no longer wear out life amid the solitude of these surrounding mountains, without even a chance of meriting applause or distinguishing my name.

The officer then desisted from his opposition, and, turning to my parents, asked them if it were with their consent that I was going to enlist. My mother burst into tears, and my sisters hung about me weeping; my father replied, with a deep sigh, I have

I have long experienced that it is vain to oppose the decrees of Providence. Could my persuasions have availed, he would have remained contented in these mountains; but that is now impossible, at least till he has purchased wisdom at the price of his blood. If, therefore, sir, you do not despise his youth and mien, take him with you, and let him have the advantage of your example. I have been a soldier myself, and I can assure you, with truth, that I have never seen an officer under whom I would more gladly march than yourself. Our guest made a polite reply to my father, and instantly agreed to receive me. He then pulled out a purse, and, offering it to my father, said, the common price of a recruit is now five guineas, but, so well am I satisfied with the appearance of your son, and the confidence you repose in me, that I must insist upon your accepting what is contained in this purse; you will dispose of it as you please for your mutual advantage. Before I depart to-morrow, I will give such directions as may enable him to join the regiment, which is now preparing to march. He then requested that he might retire to rest, and my father would have resigned the only bed he had in the house to his gueft; but he abfolutely refufed, and faid, Would you fhame me in the eyes of my new recruit? What is a foldier good for that cannot fleep without a bed? The time will foon arrive when I fhall think a comfortable roof and a little ftraw, an enviable luxury. I, therefore, raifed him as convenient a couch as I was able to make with heath and ftraw; and, wrapping himfelf up in his riding coat, he threw himfelf down upon it, and flept till morning. With the firft dawn of day he rofe and departed, having firft given me the directions which were neceffary to enable me to join the regiment: but, before he went, my father, who was equally charmed with his generofity and manners, preffed him to take back part of the money he had given us; this, however, he abfolutely refufed, and left us full of efteem and admiration.

I will not, gentlemen, repeat the affecting fcene I had to undergo in taking leave of my family and friends. It pierced me to the very heart; and then, for the firft time, I almoft repented at being fo near the accomplifhment of my wifhes. I was, however, engaged, and determined to fulfil my engagement; I, therefore, tore myfelf from my family, having, with difficulty, prevailed

vailed upon my father to accept of part of the money I had received for my enrolment. I will not trefpafs upon your time to defcribe the various emotions which I felt at the crowd of new fenfations, which entered my mind along our march. I arrived without an accident at London, the fplendid capital of this kingdom; but I could not there reftrain my aftonifhment, to fee an immenfe people talking of wounds, of death, of battles, fieges, and conquefts, in the midft of feafts, and balls, and puppet-fhows; and calmly devoting thoufands of their fellow-creatures to perifh by famine or the fword, while they confidered the lofs of a dinner, or the endurance of a fhower, as an exertion too great for human fortitude.

I foon embarked, and arrived, without any other accident than an horrible ficknefs, at the place of our deftination in America. Here I joined my gallant officer, colonel Simmons, who had performed the voyage in another fhip.—Mifs Simmons, who was prefent at this narration, feemed to be much interefted at this mention of her own name; fhe, however, did not exprefs her feelings, and the ftranger proceeded with his ftory.— This gentleman was, with juftice, the moft beloved, and the moft deferving to be fo, of any officer I have ever known. Inflexible in every thing that concerned the honour of the service, he never pardoned wilful misbehaviour, because he knew that it was incompatible with military discipline; yet, when obliged to punish, he did it with such reluctance, that he seemed to suffer almost as much as the criminal. But, if his reason imposed this just and necessary severity, his heart had taught him another lesson in respect to the private distresses of his men. He visited them in their sicknesses, relieved their miseries, and was a niggard of nothing but human blood;—but I ought to correct myself in that expression, for he was rashly lavish of his own, and to that we owe his untimely loss.

I had not been long in America before the colonel, who was perfectly acquainted with the language and manners of the savage tribes that border upon the British colonies, was sent upon an embassy to one of their nations, for the purpose of soliciting their alliance with Britain. It may, perhaps, be not uninteresting to you, gentlemen, and to this my honourable little master, to hear some account of a people whose manners and customs are so much the reverse of what you see at home. As

my

my worthy officer, therefore, contented with my affiduity and improvement in military knowledge, permitted me to have the honour of attending him, I will defcribe fome of the moſt curious facts which I was witnefs to.

You have, doubtlefs, heard many accounts of the furprizing increafe of the Englifh colonies in America; and, when we reflect that it is fcarcely an hundred years fince fome of them were eſtabliſhed, it muſt be confeſſed that they have made rapid improvements in clearing the ground of woods and bringing it to cultivation. Yet, much as they have already done, the country is yet an immenfe foreſt, except immediately upon the coaſts. Theſe foreſts extend on every fide to a diſtance that no human fagacity or obfervation has been able to determine. They abound in every fpecies of tree which you fee in England, to which may be added a great variety more which are unknown with us. Under their fhade is generally found a rich luxurious herbage, which ferves for paſture to a thoufand herds of animals. Here are feen elks, a kind of deer of the largeſt fize, and buffaloes, a fpecies of wild ox, by thouſands, and even horſes, which, having been originally

ginally brought over by the Spaniards have escaped from their settlements and multiplied in the woods.

Dear, said Tommy, that must be a fine country, indeed, where horses run wild: why a man might have one for nothing. And yet, said Mr. Merton, it would be but of little use for a person to have a wild horse, who is not able to manage a tame one.

Tommy made no answer to his father, and the man proceeded:—But the greatest curiosity of all this country is, in my opinion, the various tribes or nations which inhabit it. Bred up from their infancy to a life of equal hardiness with the wild animals, they are almost as robust in their constitutions. These various tribes inhabit little villages which generally are seated upon the banks of rivers, and, though they cultivate small portions of land around their towns, they seek the greater part of their subsistence from the chace. In their persons they are rather tall and slender, but admirably well proportioned and active, and their colour is a pale red, exactly resembling copper. Thus accustomed to roam about the woods, and brave the inclemencies of the weather, as well as continually exposed

to

to the attacks of their enemies, they acquire a degree of courage and fortitude which can scarcely be conceived. It is nothing to them to pass whole days without a morsel of food, to lie whole nights upon the bare damp ground, and to swim the widest rivers in the depth of winter. Money, indeed, and the greater part of what we call the conveniences of life, they are unacquainted with; nor can they conceive that one man should serve another merely because he has a few pieces of shining metal; they imagine that the only just distinctions arise from superior courage and bodily perfections, and therefore these alone are able to engage their esteem. I shall never forget the contempt which one of their chiefs expressed at seeing an officer who was rather corpulent at the head of his men: What fools, said he, are these Europeans, to be commanded by a man who is so unwieldy that he can neither annoy his enemies nor defend his friends, and who is only fit to be a scullion! When they are at peace, they exercise the virtue of hospitality to a degree that might shame more polished nations: if a stranger arrives at any of their towns, he enters into the first habitation he pleases, and is sure to be entertained with all

all the family poſſeſs. In this manner he might journey from one end of the continent to the other, and never fail a friendly reception.

But, if their manners are gentle in peace, they are more dreadful when provoked than all the wildeſt animals of the foreſt. Bred up from infancy to ſuffer no reſtraint, and to give an unbounded looſe to all their paſſions, they know not what it is to forgive an injury. They love their tribe with a degree of affection that is totally unknown in every other country; for that they are ready to ſuffer every hardſhip and danger; wounds, and pain, and death, they deſpiſe, as often as the intereſt of their country is concerned; but the ſame attachment renders them implacable and unforgiving to all their enemies: in ſhort, they ſeem to have all the virtues and the vices of the ancient Spartans.

To one of theſe tribes, called the Ottigamies, was Colonel Simmons ſent ambaſſador, accompanied by a few more officers, and ſome private men, among whom I had the honour to be included. We purſued our march, for ſeveral days, through foreſts which ſeemed to be of equal duration with the world itſelf. Sometimes we were

ſhrouded

shrouded in such obscurity from the thickness of the covert, that we could scarcely see the light of Heaven; sometimes we emerged into spacious meadows, bare of trees, and covered with the most luxuriant herbage, on which were feeding immense herds of buffaloes: these, as soon as they snuffed the approach of men, which they are capable of doing even at a considerable distance, ran with precipitation into the surrounding woods. Many, however, fell beneath our attack, and served us for food during our journey. At length, we came to a wide and rapid river, upon whose banks we found a party of friendly savages, with some of whom we embarked upon canoes made of the bark of trees, to proceed to the country of the Ottigamies.

After three days incessant rowing, we entered a spacious lake, upon whose banks were encamped a considerable part of the nation we sought. As we approached the shore, they saluted us with a volley of balls from their muskets, which whistled just above our heads without producing mischief. I and several of the soldiers instantly seized our arms, imagining it to be an hostile attack; but our leader quieted our apprehensions by informing us that this was

E 5   only

only a friendly falute with which a nation of warriors received and welcomed their allies. We landed, and were inftantly conducted to the affembly of the chiefs, who were fitting upon the ground, without external pomp or ceremony, with their arms befide them; but there was in their countenances and eyes an expreffion of ferocious grandeur which would have daunted the boldeft European. Yes, gentlemen, I have feen the greateft and moft powerful men in my own country; I have feen them adorned with every external circumftance of drefs, and pomp, and equipage, to infpire refpect; but never did I fee any thing which fo completely awed the foul as the angry fcowl and fiery glance of a favage American.

As foon as our leader entered the circle, he produced the calumet or pipe of peace. This is the univerfal mark of friendfhip and alliance among all the barbarous nations of America; and he that bears it, is confidered with fo much refpect, that his perfon is always fafe. This calumet is nothing but a long and flender pipe, ornamented with the moft lively and beautiful feathers, which are ingenioufly fixed along the tube. The bole is compofed of a peculiar kind of reddifh marble, and filled

with

with scented herbs and tobacco. Colonel Simmons lighted his pipe with great solemnity, and turning the bole first towards the heavens, then to the earth, then in a circle round him, he began to smoke. In the mean time the whole assembly sat with mute attention, waiting to hear his proposals: for, though we call them savages, yet in some respects, they well deserve to be imitated by more refined nations. In all their meetings and assemblies, the greatest order and regularity prevail; whoever rises to speak, is sure of being patiently heard to the end without the least interruption. Our leader then began to harangue them in their own language, with which he was well acquainted. I did not understand what past, but it was afterwards explained to me, that he set before their eyes the injuries they had mutually received from the French and the tribes in their alliance.. He told them that their great father, for so these people call the king of Britain, had taken up the hatchet of war, and was sending an innumerable band of warriors to punish the insults of his enemies.. He told them that he had ordered him to visit the Ottigamies, his dutiful children, and smoke with them the pipe of peace. He invited their young men

men to join the warriors that came from beyond the ocean, and who were marching to bury the bones of their brethren, who had been killed by their mutual foes. When he had concluded, he flung upon the ground a curious string of shells which is called the belt of Wampum. This is a neceſſary circumſtance in all the treaties made with theſe tribes. Whoever comes as an ambaſſador brings one with him to preſent to the people whoſe friendſhip is ſolicited, and if the belt is accepted, the propoſed alliance is conſidered as entered into. As ſoon as our leader had finiſhed, a chief of a ſtature ſuperior to the common race of men, and of a moſt determined look, jumped into the middle of the aſſembly, and, taking up the belt, cried out in their language: Let us march, my brethren, with the young men of our great father. Let us dig up the hatchet of war, and revenge the bones of our countrymen. They lie unburied, and cry to us for vengeance. We will not be deaf to their cries; we will ſhake off all delays; we will approve ourſelves worthy of our anceſtors. We will drink the blood of our enemies, and ſpread a feaſt of carnage for the fowls of the air and the wild
                                        beaſts

beasts of the forest. This resolution was universally approved by the whole nation, who consented to the war with a ferocious joy. The assembly was then dissolved, and the chiefs prepared for their intended march according to the manners of their country. All the savage tribes that inhabit America are accustomed to very little cloathing. Inured to the inclemencies of the weather, and being in the constant exercise of all their limbs, they cannot bear the restraint and confinement of an European dress. The greater part of their bodies, therefore, is naked, and this they paint in various fashions to give additional terror to their looks. When the chiefs were thus prepared, they came from their tents, and the last solemnity I was witness to was dancing the dance of war, and singing the song of death. But what words can convey an adequate idea of the furious movements and expressions which animated them through the whole of this performance? Every man was armed with a kind of hatchet, which is their usual weapon in battle, and called a tomahawk. This he held in his hand, and brandished through the whole of the dreadful spectacle. As they went on, their faces kindled into an expression

preffion of anger which would have daunted the boldeft fpectator. Their geftures feemed to be infpired by frantic rage and implacable animofity. They moved their bodies with the moft violent agitations, and it was eafy to fee they reprefented all the circumftances of a real combat. They seemed to be engaged in clofe or diftant battle, and brandifhed their weapons with fo much fury, that you would have imagined they were going every inftant to hew each other to pieces; nor would it have been poffible, even for the performers themfelves of this terrific dance, to have avoided mutual wounds and flaughter, had they not been endued with that extraordinary activity which is peculiar to favage nations. By intervals they increafed the horid folemnity of the exhibition, by uttering yells that would have pierced an European ear with horror. I have feen rage and fury under various forms, and in different parts of the globe, but I muft confefs, that every thing I have feen elfewhere is feeble and contemptible when compared with this day's fpectacle. When the whole was finifhed, they entertained us at a public feftival in their cabins, and when we departed, difmift us with thefe expreffive wifhes; they prayed

that

that the Great Spirit would favour us with a profperous voyage; that he would give us an unclouded fky and fmooth waters by day, and that we might lie down at night on a beaver blanket, enjoying uninterrupted fleep and pleafant dreams; and that we might find continual protection under the great pipe of peace.—I have been thus particular, faid the highlander, in defcribing the circumftances of this embaffy, becaufe you have not difdained to hear the ftory of my adventures; and I thought that this defcription of a people fo totally unlike all you have been accuftomed to in Europe might not prove entirely uninterefting.

We are much obliged to you, faid Mr. Barlow, for all thefe curious particulars, which are perfectly conformable to all I have heard and read upon the fubject. Nor can I confider, without a certain degree of admiration, the favage grandeur of man in his moft fimple ftate. The paffion for revenge, which marks the character of all uncivilized nations, is certainly to be condemned. But it is one of the conftant prejudices of their education, and many of thofe that call themfelves refined, have more

to

to blush at, in that respect, than they are aware of. Few, I am afraid, even in the most refined state of society, have arrived at that sublime generosity, which is able to forgive the injuries of its fellow-creatures, when it has the power to repay them; and I see many around me, that are disgraced by the vices of uncivilized Americans, without a claim to their virtues.

I will not fatigue your ears, continued the highlander, with a recital of all the events I was engaged in, during the progress of the war. The description of blood and carnage is always disagreeable to a humane mind; and though the perversity of mankind may sometimes render war a necessary evil, the remembrance of its mischiefs is always painful. I will only mention one event, continually lamented in the annals of this country, because it is connected with the untimely fate of my noble friend and gallant leader.

It was determined by those who governed, that we should march through the woods upon a distant expedition against the French. The conduct of this enterprize was given to a brave but rash commander, totally unacquainted with the people he had to oppose, and unskilled in the nature of a savage

war.

war. We therefore began our march through the same tractless wilds I have described. We proceeded for several days, without any other difficulties than the nature of the country itself produced, and without seeing the face of an enemy. It was in vain that officers of the greatest experience, and particularly my worthy colonel, suggested to our commander the necessity of using every precaution against a dangerous and insidious foe. War is not managed, amid the forests of America, in the same manner as it is conducted upon the plains of Europe. The temper of the people there conspires with the nature of the country, to render it a continual scene of stratagems and surprize. Unincumbered with tents, or baggage, or numerous trains of artillery, the hostile warriors set out in small and chosen parties, with nothing but their arms, and are continually upon the watch to deceive their enemies. Long experience has taught them a degree of sagacity in traversing the woods, which to us is inconceivable. Neither the widest rivers, nor the most extensive forests, can retard them for an instant. A march of a thousand miles is scarcely to them a greater difficulty than the passage of an European

army

army between two neighbouring towns. The woods themselves afford them a continual supply of provisions, in the various animals which they kill by the chace. When they are near their enemies, they frequently lurk all day in thickets, for fear of a discovery, and pursue their march by night. Hundreds of them sometimes pursue their course in the same line, treading only in each other's steps, and the last of the party carefully covers over the impressions which his fellows have made. When they are thus upon the point of accomplishing their purpose, the very necessities of nature are unheeded: they cease to fire upon the beasts of the forest, lest it should alarm the foe; they feed upon roots or the bark of trees, or pass successive days in a perfect abstinence from food. All this our colonel represented to the general, and conjured him, with the strongest entreaties, not to hazard the safety of our army by an incautious progress. He advised him to send out numerous detachments to beat the bushes and examine the woods; and offered himself to secure the march of the army. But presumption is always blind: our general was unacquainted with any other than

European

European warfare, and could not conceive that naked savages would dare to attack an army of two thousand disciplined troops. One morning the way before us appeared more intricate and obscure than common; the forests did not as usual consist of lofty trees, which afford a tolerably clear prospect between their trunks, but were composed of creeping bushes and impervious thickets. The army marched as usual with the vain ostentation of military discipline, but totally unprepared for the dreadful scene which followed. At length we entered a gloomy valley, surrounded on every side by the thickest shade, and rendered swampy by the overflowings of a little rivulet. In this situation it was impossible to continue our march without disordering our ranks; and part of the army extended itself beyond the rest, while another part of the line involuntarily fell behind. In the moment while the officers were employed in rectifying the disorder of their men, a sudden noise of musquetry was heard in front, which stretched about twenty of our men upon the field. The soldiers instinctively fired towards the part whence they were attacked, and instantly fell back in disorder. But it was equally vain to retreat or go forward, for it now ap-

appeared that we were completely hemmed in. On every fide refounded the fatal peals of fcattering fire, that thinned our ranks and extended our braveft comrades on the earth. Figure to yourfelf a fhoal of fifhes enclofed within the net, that circle in vain the fatal labyrinth in which they are involved; or rather conceive, what I have myfelf been witnefs to, an herd of deer furrounded on every fide by a band of active and unpitying hunters, that prefs and gall them on every fide, and exterminate them at leifure in their flight. Juft fuch was the fituation of our unfortunate countrymen. After a few unavailing difcharges which never annoyed a fecret enemy that fcattered death unfeen, the ranks were broken, and all fubordination loft. The ground was covered with gafping wretches, and ftained with blood; the woods refounded with cries and groans, and fruitlefs attempts of our gallant officers to rally their men and check the progrefs of the enemy. By intervals was heard, more fhrill, more dreadful than all the reft, the difmal yell of the victorious favages, that now, emboldened by their fuccefs, began to leave the covert, and hew down thofe who fled; with unrelenting cruelty. As to myfelf, the defcription which

our

our colonel had given me of their method of attack, and the precautions to be used against it, rendered me perhaps less disturbed than I should otherwise have been. I remarked that those who stood and those who fled were exposed to equal danger; those who kept their rank, and endeavoured to repel the enemy, exposed their persons to their fire and were successively shot down, as happened to most of our unfortunate officers; while those who fled frequently rushed headlong upon the very death they sought to avoid. Pierced to the heart at the sight of such a carnage of my gallant comrades, I grew indifferent to life and abandoned myself to despair; but it was a despair that neither impaired my exertions nor robbed me of the faculties of my mind. Imitate me, I cried, my gallant countrymen, and we shall yet be safe. I then directly ran to the nearest tree, and sheltered myself behind its stem; convinced that this precaution alone could secure me from the incessant vollies which darted on every side. A small number of highlanders followed my example, and, thus secured, we began to fire with more success at the enemy, who now exposed themselves with less reserve. This check seemed to astonish and confound them;

them; and had not the panic been so general, it is possible that this successful effort might have changed the fortune of the fight; for in another quarter the provincial troops that accompanied us behaved with the greatest bravery, and, though deserted by the European forces, effected their own retreat. But it was now too late to hope for victory or even safety; the ranks were broken on every side, the greater part of our officers slain or wounded, and our unfortunate general himself had expiated with his life, his fatal rashness. I cast my eyes around, and saw nothing but images of death, and horror, and frantic rage. Yet even then the safety of my noble colonel was dearer to me than my own. I sought him for some time in vain, amid the various scenes of carnage which surrounded me. At length, I discovered him at a distance, almost deserted by his men, yet still attempting to renew the fight, and heedless of the wounds which covered him. Transported with grief and passion, I immediately darted forward to offer him my feeble support; but in the very instant of my arrival, he received a straggling ball in his bosom, and tottering to a tree, supported his fainting limbs against the trunk. Just in that moment,

three

three of our savage enemies observed his situation and marked him for their prey; they raised their hideous yell, and darted upon him with the speed and fierceness of wolves. Fury then took possession of my soul; had I possessed a thousand lives I should have held them cheap in the balance:—I fired with so unerring an aim that I stretched the foremost on the earth; the second received the point of my bayonet in his breast, and fell in the pangs of death; the third, daunted with the fate of his companions, turned his steps another way. Just then an horse that had lost his rider was galloping along the wood; I bounded across the path, and, seizing him by the bridle, instantly led him to my leader, and conjured him to preserve his glorious life. He thanked me in the most affectionate manner for my friendship, but bade me preserve my own life. As to myself, said he, I do not wish to survive my country's dishonour, and even had I such a wish, the wounds I have received would render all escape impossible. If that is your resolution, said I, we will die together, for I swear by the eternal majesty of my Creator, that I will not leave you. When he saw me thus resolved, he consented to use my assistance, and with infinite

finite difficulty I seated him upon the horse, which, holding by the reins, as I was then light and active, I guided along the wood with no inconsiderable speed. Fortunately for me we were not observed by any of our savage enemies; so that flying through the thickest part of the forest, we left the danger behind, and were soon removed beyond the sight or hearing of the battle. Courage, said I, my noble leader, you are now almost in safety; and I trust you will yet preserve a life so necessary to your friends and country. He answered me with the kindest expressions, but with a feeble voice: Campbell, I have consented to fly more for the sake of preserving your life, than from any hopes of my own. But since we are at a distance from yonder dreadful scene, permit me to alight; I have consumed my small remaining forces in the way, and now I faint from loss of blood. He sunk down at this, and would have fallen, but I received him in my arms; I bore him to the next thicket, and strewing grass and leaves upon the ground, endeavoured to prepare him a bed. He thanked me again with gratitude and tenderness, and grasped my hand as he lay in the very agonies of death; for such it was, although I believed he had

only

only fainted, and long tried every ineffectual method to reſtore departed life. Thus was I deprived of the nobleſt officer and kindeſt friend that ever deſerved the attachment of a ſoldier; twenty years have now rolled over me ſince that inauſpicious day; yet it lives for ever in my remembrance, and never ſhall be blotted from my ſoul. The highlander then turned away to hide a tear which did not miſbecome his manly countenance; the company ſeemed all to ſhare his griefs, but Miſs Simmons above the reſt; however, as the natural gentleneſs of her temper was ſufficiently known, no one ſuſpected that ſhe had any particular intereſt in the relation.

I ſat till night, continued the ſtranger, ſupporting the breathleſs body of my colonel, and vainly hoping he might return to life. At length I perceived that his noble ſoul was fled for ever; my own wounds grew ſtiff and painful, and exhauſted nature required a ſupply of food. I therefore aroſe, and finding a ſpring that trickled down an hill at no great diſtance, I refreſhed myſelf by a copious draught, and waſhed the clotted blood away from the hurts I had received. I then cruſhed ſome leaves, which the inhabitants of that country imagine ſalutary, and bound them on with bandages I tore from my linen. I alfo found a few wild fruits, which paft experience had taught me were innocent, with which I allayed the pains of hunger. I then returned to the thicket, and, creeping into the thickeft part, endeavoured to compofe myfelf to reft. Strange, gentlemen, as it may appear, neither the forlorn nature of my fituation, nor the dangers with which I was befet, were fufficient to keep me awake. My wearied and exhaufted body feemed to triumph over all the agitations of my mind; and I funk into a fleep as deep and profound as that of death itfelf. I awoke next morning, with the firft rays of the fun; but, more compofed, I better underftood the difficulties in which I was involved, and the uncertainty of my efcape. I was in the midft of an immenfe defert, totally deftitute of human affiftance or fupport. Should I meet with any of my fellow-creatures, I could expect nothing but implacable cruelty; and even if I efcaped their vigilance, what method of finding fubfiftence, or of meafuring back without a guide the long and tedious march I had trodden? Hope, however, and the vigour of my conftitution, ftill fupported me. I reflected, that it is the common

mon lot of man to struggle with misfortunes; that it is cowardice to yield to evils, when present, the representation of which had not deterred me from voluntarily embracing the profession of a soldier; and that the providence of Heaven was as capable of protecting me in the forests of America, as upon my native mountains. I therefore determined to struggle with the difficulties which surrounded me to the last, and to meet my fortune like a man. Yet, as I still by intervals heard the dismal cries of the enemy, and saw their fires at a distance, I lay close till night in the obscurity of my thicket. When all was dark and still, I ventured abroad, and laid in my scanty provision of fruits and herbs, and drank again at the spring. The pain of my wounds began now to abate a little, though I suffered extremely from the cold, as I did not dare to kindle a fire, from the fear of discovering myself by its light. Three nights and days did I lead this solitary life, in continual dread of the savage parties which scouted all the woods in pursuit of stragglers, and often past so near my place of retreat, that I gave myself over for lost. At length upon the fourth evening, fancying myself a little restored, and that the activity of the enemy might be abated, I ventured out and pursued my march. I scarcely need describe the various difficulties and dangers to which I was exposed in such a journey; however I still had with me my musquet, and as my ammunition was not quite exhausted, I depended upon the woods themselves to supply me with food. I travelled the greater part of the night, involving myself still deeper in these inextricable forests; for I was afraid to pursue the direction of our former march, as I imagined the savages were dispersed along the country in pursuit of the fugitives. I therefore took a direction as nearly as I could judge parallel to the English settlements, and inclining to the South. In this manner, I forced my way along the woods all night, and with the morning had reason to think that I had advanced a considerable distance. My wounds began now to pain me afresh with this exertion, and compelled me to allow myself some repose. I chose out the thickest covert I could find, and, shrowding myself as well as I was able, was soon over-powered by sleep. I did not awake till the sun had gained the meridian, and, creeping from my retreat, beheld with some degree of terror an enormous rattle-snake

that

that was coiled up full in my way and seemed determined to oppose my passage. This animal is frequent in the southern colonies, and is the most poisonous of all the reptiles that haunt the woods. He is in length from two to six feet, beautifully variegated with different colours, but the most remarkable circumstance attending him is a natural noise that he produces with every emotion of his tail, and which occasions too his name. I soon destroyed my hissing foe, and taking courage for the first time to kindle a fire, I roasted him upon the embers, and made the most delicious meal I ever remember upon his flesh.

What, exclaimed Tommy, is it possible to eat snakes? I thought they had been all over poison. Master, replied the highlander, the want of food will reconcile us to many meats, which, we should scarcely think eatable. Nothing has surprized me more than to see the poor, in various countries, complaining of the scarcity of food, yet throwing away every year thousands of the carcases of horses, which are full as wholesome and nourishing as beef, and are in many countries preferred to it. But, in general, every animal may be eaten, and affords a salutary food; as to snakes, the

poison

poifon of them is contained in the hollow of their teeth. When they bite, they inftil their venom into the wound, which mixes with the blood, and without a timely remedy, deftroys the fufferer. But if you cut off the head, the reft of the body is not only wholefome but palatable, and I have known it eaten as a delicacy by many inhabitants of the colonies.—Thus refrefhed, therefore, I purfued my march through the fame thick, gloomy country, without meeting the leaft appearance of an human creature; and at night, I cut, with an hatchet that I had about me, fome boughs, with which I erected a temporary fhelter. The next day, as I was purfuing my march, I faw a deer bound by me, upon whofe fhoulders was fixed a fierce and deftructive animal that refembles a tiger. This creature, which is about the fize of a moderate dog, afcends the trees and hides himfelf among the branches, till a deer, or any other animal that he can mafter, paffes within his reach. He then darts himfelf with a fudden fpring, full upon the neck or fhoulder of the unfortunate animal, which he continues tearing with fo much violence, that he foon difpatches him. This was actually the cafe with the poor deer that paft me; for he had not run an hundred yards,

before

before he fell down in the agonies of death, and his deftroyer began to regale himfelf upon the prey. I inftantly faw that this was a lucky opportunity of fupplying myfelf with food for feveral days; I therefore ran towards the animal, and by a violent fhout made him abandon his victim and retire growling into the woods. I then kindled a fire with leaves and fticks, and, cutting off a large flice of venifon, I plentifully refrefhed myfelf for my journey. I then packed up as much of the moft flefhy parts of the body as I could conveniently carry, and abandoned the reft to wild beafts. In this manner did I march for feveral days, without wanting food, or feeing any probable end of my fatigues. At length I found a lofty mountain before me, which I determined to afcend, imagining that fuch an elevation might enable me to make fome ufeful difcoveries in refpect to the nature of the country I had to traverfe, and perhaps prefent me with fome appearances of cultivation or inhabitants. I therefore afcended with infinite fatigue a rough and ftony afcent of feveral miles, in which I was frequently obliged to clamber up pointed rocks, and work my way along the edge of dangerous precipices. I however arrived with-

F 4. out

out an accident at the top, which was entirely bare of trees, and looking round me beheld a wild and defert country extended to a prodigious diftance. Far as my eye could reach, I difcovered nothing but forefts on every fide but one. There the country feemed to be more open, though equally uncultivated, and I faw meadows and favannahs opening one beyond another, bounded at length by a fpacious river, whofe end and beginning were equally concealed from my eye. I was now fo weary of this folitary kind of life, that I began to confider the inhabitants themfelves with lefs apprehenfion; befides, I thought myfelf out of danger of meeting with the hoftile tribes: and all thefe people, unlefs irritated by injuries or ftimulated by revenge are perhaps lefs ftrangers to the rights of hofpitality than any civilized nation. I, therefore, reflected, that by directing my courfe to the river, and following the direction of its waters, I fhould have the greateft probability of meeting with fome of my fellow-creatures; as the natives build their villages near lakes and ftreams, and choofe their banks as a refidence, when they are employed in hunting.

I there-

I therefore defcended the mountain, and entered the level diftrict which I faw before me. I marched along an open campaign country for feveral hours, covered over with a rank fpecies of grafs, and beheld numerous herds of buffaloes grazing all around. It was here that an accident befel me, which I will relate for its fingularity, both in refpect to the dangers I incurred and my method of efcape. As I was thus journeying on I difcovered a prodigious light that feemed to efface the fun itfelf, and ftreak the fkies with an angry kind of illumination. I looked round me to difcover the caufe of this ftrange appearance, and beheld, with equal horror and aftonifhment, that the whole country behind was in flames. In order to explain this event, I muft obferve, that all the plains in America produce a rank, luxuriant vegetation, the juices of which are exhaufted by the heat of the fummer's fun: it is then as inflammable as ftraw or fodder; and when a cafual fpark of fire communicates with it, the flame frequently drives before the wind for miles together, and confumes every thing it meets. This was actually the cafe at prefent; far as my eye could reach, the country was all in flames: a powerful wind added

added frefh fury to the fire, and drove it on with a degree of fwiftnefs which precluded all poffibility of flight. I muft confefs that I was ftruck with horror at the fudden approach of a death, fo new, fo dreadful, fo unexpected. I faw it was in vain to fly; the flaming line extended for feveral miles on every fide, and advanced with fuch velocity that I confidered my fate as inevitable. I looked round me with a kind of mute defpair, and began to envy the fate of my comrades who had fallen by honourable wounds in battle. Already did the conflagration fcorch me in its approach, accompanied by clouds of fmoke that almoft fuffocated me with their baneful vapour. In this extremity, fortune prefented to my mind an inftantaneous thought, which, perhaps, was the only poffible method of efcape. I confidered that nothing could ftop the conflagration but an actual want of matter to continue it; and, therefore, by fetting fire to the vegetables before me, I might follow my own path in fafety. I hope, gentlemen, that during the courfe of a long life, you will never have occafion to experience the pleafure which the firft glance of this expedient afforded to my mind. I faw myfelf fnatched, beyond

yond expectation, from a strange and painful death, and instantly pulled out, with a trembling hand, the flint and steel upon which my preservation was to depend. I struck a light and presently kindled the driest grass before me: the conflagration spread along the country; the wind drove it on with inconceivable fury, and I saw the path of my deliverance open before my eyes. In a few seconds a considerable vacancy was burnt before me, which I traversed with the speed of a man that flies from instant death. My feet were scorched with the glowing soil, and several times had I been nearly suffocated with the drift of the pursuing smoke; but every step I made, convinced me of the certainty of my escape, and, in a little time, I stopped to consider at leisure the conflagration I had avoided; which, after proceeding to the point whence I set out, was extinguished, as I had foreseen, and delivered me from all apprehension.

I declare, said Tommy, this is the most extraordinary thing I ever heard; and yet I can easily conceive it, for I once saw some men set fire to the heath and furzes upon the common, and they burnt so furiously that

that I was quite afraid to come near the flame.

I purfued my way, continued the highlander, over the fmoking foil, which I had rendered bare to a confiderable extent, and lodged at night, as ufual, under fome boughs which I ftuck up to defend me. In the morning I fet out again, and foon arrived at a fpacious lake, upon whofe banks I could plainly difcern the figns of an American encampment. I hefitated fome time, whether I fhould again conceal myfelf in the woods, or deliver myfelf up to their mercy. But I confidered that it was impoffible long to continue this wandering life; and that, in the end, I muft have recourfe to fome of thofe favage tribes for affiftance. What, therefore, muft be done at laft, it was fruitlefs to delay; I had every reafon to imagine that the people before me muft either be favourable to Great Britain, or at leaft indifferent to the war, and in either cafe, from the experience I poffeft of the manners of the natives, I did not think I had much to fear. I, therefore, determined to hazard every thing upon the probability of a favourable reception, and, collecting all my refolution, I marched boldly forward,

forward, and soon arrived at the encampment. As soon as I entered the village the women and children gathered round me with the curiosity natural to mankind at the sight of an unaccustomed object. I formed a favourable conjecture from this apparent ignorance of Europeans, and walking on with a composed step and steady countenance, I at length entered into one of the largest cabins I could find. When I was within, I saw a venerable old man, whom I took to be a chief from his appearance, sitting at his ease upon the ground, and smoking. I saluted him with all the courtesy I was able, and placed myself upon the ground, at some little distance, waiting with inward anxiety, but external composure, for him to begin the conversation. After he had eyed me for some time with fixt attention, but without either sternness or anger, he calmly took the pipe from his mouth and presented it to me. I received it with infinite satisfaction, for, as I have before remarked, this is always with the American tribes the firmest pledge of peace and a friendly reception. When we had thus been seated for some time in mutual contemplation of each other, he asked me, in a dialect which I understood tolerably well,

well, to eat. I did not think it prudent to refuse any offered civility, and therefore accepted the offer; and, in a little time, a young woman, who was in the back part of the hut, set before me some broiled fish and parched maize. After I had eaten, my friendly host inquired into my country and the reasons of my visit. I was just enough acquainted with the language he spoke to be able to understand him, and to give an intelligible, though imperfect, answer. I therefore explained to him, as well as I was able, that I had crost the great water, with the warriors of the king of Britain; that we had been compelled to take up the hatchet against the French and their allies, and that we had actually set out upon an expedition against their colonies; but that we had been surprized by a lurking party in the woods; that in the confusion of the fight I had been separated from the rest, and had wandered several days through the woods in search of my comrades; and that now seeing the tents of my brethren, the red men, I had come to visit them, and smoke the pipe of peace in their company. All this I with some difficulty explained to my entertainer, who listened to me with great attention, and then bade me welcome in the

the name of his nation, which he told me was called the Saukies; he added that their young men were difperfed through the woods, hunting the deer and buffalo; but they would foon return loaded with provifions, and in the mean time I might fhare his cabin, and fuch provifions as he could command. I thanked him for his offer, and remained feveral days in his hut, always entertained with the fame hofpitality, until the return of the young men from hunting. They came at laft, in feveral boats, along the lake, bringing with them a confiderable quantity of wild beafts which they had killed. I was received by all the tribe with the fame hofpitality I had experienced from the old chief; and, as it was neceffary to gain their friendfhip as much as poffible, I joined them in all their hunting and fifhing parties, and foon acquired a confiderable degree of fkill in both.

Hunting itfelf has fomething cruel in the practice; it is a fpecies of war which we wage with brute animals for their fpoils; but if ever it can be confidered as excufeable, it is in thefe favage nations, who have recourfe to it for their fubfiftence. They are active, bold, and dexterous, to fuch a degree in all thefe exercifes, that none of the wild

wild animals they attack have the smallest chance of escape. Their parties generally consist of almost all the youth of their nation, who go in a body to particular districts where they know game is plentiful. Their common method is, when they are arrived at a spot which abounds in deer or buffaloes, to disperse themselves through the woods; and then, alarming the beasts in the neighbourhood, they drive them with shouts and dogs towards some common place, which is always in the middle of all their parties. When they have thus rouzed their prey, the various squadrons gradually advance towards the centre till they unite in a circle, and inclose a prodigious number of frightened animals. They then attack them either with fire-arms or arrows, and shoot them down successively. By these means they are sure, in a single day, to destroy a prodigious number of different beasts. But it sometimes happens, that while they are engaged in the chace of other animals, they become a prey themselves to their enemies; who take this method of surprizing them in the woods and gratifying their resentment. This was actually the case with my friends the Saukies, and produced a surprizing event; the consequence

of

of which was my return to the English colonies in safety.

The Saukies had been long at war with the Iroquese, a powerful tribe of Northern Americans in the interest of the French. The Iroquese had received intelligence of the situation of the Saukies encampment, and determined to surprize them. For this purpose, a thousand warriors set out by a secret march, through the woods, and travelled with the silence and celerity which are peculiar to all these nations. When they had nearly approached the hunting grounds of their enemies, they happened to be discovered upon their march, by four warriors of another nation, who instantly suspected their design, and, running with greater diligence than it was possible so large a body could make, arrived at the encampment of the Saukies, and informed them of the near approach of their enemies. A great council was instantly assembled to deliberate upon the choice of proper measures for their defence. As they were incumbered with their families, it was impracticable to retreat with safety; and it seemed equally difficult to resist so large a force with inferior numbers. While they were in this uncertainty, I considered the

nature

nature of their situation, and had the good fortune to find out a resource, which being communicated to my friend the chief, and adopted by the nation, was the means of their safety. I observed that the passage to the Saukie camp for the Iroquese lay along a narrow slip of land, which extended for near a mile between two lakes. I, therefore, advised the Saukies to cast up a strong barrier at the end of the passage; which I shewed them how to strengthen with ditches, palisades, and some of the improvements of European fortification. Their number of warriors amounted to about four hundred; these I divided into equal parts, and leaving one to defend the lines, I placed the other in ambuscade along the neighbouring woods. Scarcely were these dispositions finished before the Iroquese appeared, and imagining they were rushing upon an unguarded foe, entered the defile without hesitation. As soon as the whole body was thus imprudently engaged, the other party of the Saukies started from their hiding places, and running to the entrance of the strait, threw up in an instant another fortification, and had the satisfaction to see the whole force of their enemies thus circumvented and caught in a trap. The Iroquese quefe foon perceived the difficulty and danger of efcape. They however behaved with that extraordinary compofure which is the peculiar characteriftic of this people on every occafion. The lakes were at that time frozen over, yet not fo hard as to permit them to effect a paffage over the ice, and though a thaw fucceeded in a fhort time, it was equally impracticable to pafs by fwimming, or on rafts. Three days therefore the Iroquefe remained quiet in this difagreeable fituation; and, as if they had nothing to apprehend, diverted themfelves all this time with fifhing. On the fourth morning they judged the ice fufficiently diffolved to attempt their efcape; and, therefore, cutting down fome trees which grew upon the ftrait, they formed them into rafts and embarked their whole force. But this could not be done without the knowledge of the Saukies, who difpatched a confiderable body of warriors to oppofe their landing. It is unneceffary to relate all the horrid particulars of the engagement which enfued; I will only mention that the Iroquefe at length effected their landing with the lofs of half their number, and retreated precipitately to their own country, leaving behind them all the furs and fkins which they

they had taken in their hunting. The share I had had in this succefs gained me the friendſhip of all the nation; and, at my defire, they fent fome of their young men to guide me through the woods to the Engliſh ſettlements, and took their leave of me with every expreſſion of eſteem, and a conſiderable preſent of valuable furs.

Theſe, gentlemen, are the moſt important and intereſting of my adventures; and as I have already treſpaſſed too long upon your patience, I ſhall haſten to conclude my ſtory. After this, I was employed in various parts of America and the Weſt Indies, during the reſt of the war. I ſuffered hardſhips and difficulties innumerable, and acquired, as my father had foretold, a little wiſdom at the price of a conſiderable quantity of blood. When the war was ended, I found myſelf nearly in the ſame ſituation as I began, except the preſent of my friendly Americans, which I had turned into money and remitted to England. I, therefore, now began to feel my military enthuſiaſm abated, and having permiſſion to leave the ſervice, I embraced that opportunity of returning to my country, fully determined to ſpend the remainder of my life amid my family and friends. I found my

father

father and mother still living, who received me in the fondest manner. I then employed the little fund I had acquired to stock a farm, which I hired in the neighbourhood, and where I imagined my care and industry would be sufficient to ensure us all a comfortable subsistence. Some little time after, I married a virtuous and industrious young woman, the mother of the unfortunate children who are so much indebted to your bounty. For some time I made a shift to succeed tolerably well: but at length the distresses of my country increasing, I found myself involved in the deepest poverty. Several years of uncommon severity destroyed my cattle, which is the chief support of the highlanders, and rotted the scanty crops, which were to supply us with food, upon the ground. I cannot accuse myself of either voluntary unthriftiness or neglect of my business; but there are some situations in which it seems impossible for human exertion to stem the torrent of misfortune. But wherefore should I give pain to such kind and worthy benefactors, by a detail of all the miseries which I, and many of my poor countrymen, have endured?— I will therefore only mention, that after having suffered, I think, every distress which human

human nature is equal to support; after having seen my tender parents, and last, my dear, unfortunate wife, perish by the hardships of our situation, I took the resolution of for ever abandoning a country which seemed incapable of supporting its inhabitants. I thought that the milder climate and more fertile soil of America might perhaps enable a wretched wanderer, who asked no more than food for his starving children, to drag on, a little longer, a miserable life. With this idea, I sold the remainder of my stock, and after having paid whatever was due to my landlord, I found I had just enough to transport myself and family into eternal banishment. I reached a sea-port town, and embarked with my children on board a ship that was setting sail for Philadelphia. But the same ill fortune seemed still to accompany my steps; for a dreadful storm arose, which, after having tossed our vessel during several days, wrecked us at length upon the coast. All the crew, indeed, escaped, and with infinite difficulty I saved these dear, but miserable infants, who now accompany me; but when I reflect upon my situation, in a distant country, without resources, friends, or hopes, I am almost inclined to think, that we might all

have

have been happier in the bosom of the ocean.

Here the highlander finished his story, and all the company were affected with the recital of his distresses. They all endeavoured to comfort him with the kindest expressions and promises of assistance, but Miss Simmons, after she had with some difficulty composed herself enough to speak, asked the man if his name was not Andrew Campbell. The highlander answered with some surprize, it was. Then, said she, you will find that you have a friend, whom, as yet, you are not acquainted with, who has both the ability and the will to serve you. That friend, added she, seeing all the company were astonished, is no other than my uncle. That Colonel Simmons, whom you have described with so much feeling and affection, was brother to my father, and consequently uncle to myself. It is no wonder that the memory of such a man should be venerated by all his relations. I have often heard my uncle speak of his untimely death as the greatest misfortune which ever happened to our family; and I have often seen him read, with tears in his eyes, many of his brother's letters, in which he speaks with

the

the greatest affection of his faithful highlander, Andrew Campbell.

At these words the poor highlander, unable to repress the strong emotions of his mind, sprang forward in a sudden transport of joy, and, without confideration of circumstances, caught Miss Simmons in his arms, exclaiming at the same time, Praised be God for this happy and unexpected meeting! Blessed be my shipwreck itself, that has given me an opportunity of seeing, before I die, some of the blood of my dear and worthy colonel! and perceiving Miss Simmons confused at this abrupt and unexpected salutation, he added, in the most respectful manner: Pardon me, my honoured young lady, for the improper liberty I have taken; but I was not master of myself to find, at a time when I thought myself the most forlorn and miserable of the human race, that I was in company with the nearest relation of the man, that, after my own father, I have always loved and reverenced most. Miss Simmons answered, with the greatest affability, that she freely excused the warmth of his affection; and that she would that very day acquaint her uncle with this extraordinary event; who, she did not doubt, would come over with the greatest expedition to see a person whom he knew so well by name, and who could inform him of so many particulars of her uncle.

And now the company being separated, Tommy, who had listened with silent attention to the story of the highlander, took an opportunity of following Mr. Barlow, who was walking out; and when he perceived they were alone, he looked at him as if he had some weighty matter to disclose, but was unable to give it utterance. Mr. Barlow, therefore, turned towards him with the greatest kindness, and, taking him tenderly by the hand, inquired what he wished. Indeed, sir, answered Tommy, almost crying, I am scarcely able to tell you. But I have been a very bad and ungrateful boy, and I am afraid you no longer have the same affection for me.

Mr. BARLOW.

If you are sensible of your faults, my little friend, that is a very great step towards amending them. Let me therefore know what it is, the recollection of which distresses you so much, and if it is in my power to assist in making you easy, there is nothing, I am sure, which I shall be inclined to refuse you.

TOMMY.

Tommy.

Oh! fir, your speaking to me with so much goodness hurts me a great deal more than if you were to be very angry. For when people are angry and passionate, one does not so much mind what they say. But when you speak with so much kindness it seems to pierce me to the very heart, because I know I have not deserved it.

Mr. Barlow.

But if you are sensible of having committed any faults, you may resolve to behave so well for the future, that you may deserve every body's friendship and esteem. Few people are so perfect as not to err sometimes; and if you are convinced of your errors, you will be more cautious how you give way to them a second time.

Tommy.

Indeed, sir, I am very happy to hear you say so—I will then tell you every thing which lies so heavy upon my mind. You must know then, sir, that, although I have lived so long with you, and, during all that time, you have taken so much pains to improve me in every thing, and teach me to act well to every body, I had no sooner quitted

quitted your fight, than I became, I think, a worfe boy than ever I was before.

Mr. Barlow.

But why do you judge fo feverely of yourfelf, as to think you were become worfe than ever? Perhaps you have been a little thoughtlefs and giddy, and thefe are faults which I cannot with truth fay you were ever free from.

Tommy.

No, fir, what I have been guilty of is infinitely worfe than ever. I have always been very giddy and very thoughtlefs; but I never imagined I could have been the moft infolent and ungrateful boy in the world.

Mr. Barlow.

You frighten me, my little friend.—Is it poffible you can have committed actions that deferve fo harfh a name?

Tommy.

You fhall judge yourfelf, fir; for now I have begun, I am determined to tell you all. You know, fir, that when I firft came to you, I had an high opinion of myfelf for being born a gentleman, and a very great contempt for every body in an inferior station.

Mr. BARLOW.

I muſt confeſs you have always had ſome tendency to both thoſe follies.

TOMMY.

Yes, ſir; but you have ſo often laughed at me upon the ſubject, and ſhown me the folly of people's imagining themſelves better than others, without any merit of their own, that I was grown a little wiſer. Beſides, I have ſo often obſerved that thoſe I deſpiſed could do a variety of things which I was ignorant of, while thoſe who are vain of being gentlemen can do nothing uſeful or ingenious, that I had begun to be aſhamed of my folly. But ſince I came home, I kept company with a great many fine young gentlemen and ladies that thought themſelves ſuperior to all the reſt of the world, and uſed to deſpiſe every one elſe, and they have made me forget every thing I learned before.

Mr. BARLOW.

Perhaps then I was miſtaken, when I taught you that the greateſt merit any perſon could have, is to be good and uſeful;

theſe

thefe fine young gentlemen and ladies may be wifer, and have given you better leſſons. If that is the cafe, you will have great reaſon to rejoice that you have changed ſo much for the better.

TOMMY.

No, ſir, no; I never thought them either good or wife; for they know nothing but how to dreſs their hair and buckle their ſhoes. But they perſuaded me that it was neceſſary to be polite, and talked to me ſo often upon the ſubject, that I could not help believing them.

Mr. BARLOW.

I am very glad to hear that; it is neceſſary for every body to be polite. They therefore, I ſuppoſe, inſtructed you to be more obliging and civil in your manners than ever you were before. Inſtead of doing you any hurt, this will be the greateſt improvement you can receive.

TOMMY.

No, ſir, quite the contrary—Inſtead of teaching me to be civil and obliging, they have made me ruder and worſe behaved than ever I was before.

Mr.

Mr. BARLOW.

If that is the case, I fear these fine young gentlemen and ladies undertook to teach you more than they understood themselves.

TOMMY.

Indeed, sir, I am of the same opinion myself. But I did not think so then, and, therefore, I did whatever I observed them do, and talked in the same manner as I heard them talk. They used to be always laughing at Harry Sandford; and I grew so foolish that I did not choose to keep company with him any longer.

Mr. BARLOW.

That was a pity, because I am convinced he really loves you. However, it is of no great consequence, for he has employment enough at home; and, however ingenious you may be, I do not think that he will learn how to manage his land, or raise food, from your conversation. It will, therefore, be better for him to converse with farmers, and leave you to the society of gentlemen. Indeed, this, I know, has always been his taste, and had not your father prest him very much to accompany you home, he

would

would have liked much better to avoid the visit. However, I will inform him that you have gained other friends, and advise him, for the future, to avoid your company.

TOMMY.

Oh, sir! I did not think you could be so cruel. I love Harry Sandford better than any other boy in the world, and I shall never be happy till he forgives me all my bad behaviour, and converses with me again as he used to do.

Mr. BARLOW.

But then, perhaps, you may lose the acquaintance of all those polite young gentlemen and ladies.

TOMMY.

I care very little about that, sir. But, I fear, I have behaved so ill, that he never will be able to forgive me and love me as he did formerly.

Tommy then went on, and repeated with great exactness the story of his insolence and ingratitude, which had so great an effect upon him, that he burst into tears and cried a considerable time. He then concluded with asking Mr. Barlow if he thought Harry would be ever able to forgive him.

Mr. BARLOW.

I cannot conceal from you, my little friend, that you have acted very ill indeed in this affair. However, if you are really ashamed of all your past conduct, and determined to act better, I do not doubt that so generous and good-natured a boy as Harry is, will forgive you all.

TOMMY.

O, sir, I should be the happiest creature in the world—Will you be so kind as to bring him here to-day, and you shall see how I will behave?

Mr. BARLOW.

Softly, Tommy, softly. What is Harry to come here for? Have you not insulted and abused him, without reason; and, at last, proceeded so far as to strike him, only because he was giving you the best advice, and endeavouring to preserve you from danger? Can you imagine that any human being will come to you in return for such treatment? at least till you have convinced him that you are ashamed of your passion and injustice, and that he may expect better usage for the future.

TOMMY.

TOMMY.

What then must I do, sir?

Mr. BARLOW.

If you want any future connection with Harry Sandford, it is your business to go to him and tell him so.

TOMMY.

What, sir, go to a farmer's, to expose myself before all his family?

Mr. BARLOW.

Just now you told me you were ready to do every thing, and yet you cannot take the trouble of visiting your friend at his own house. You then imagine that a person does not expose himself by acting wrong, but by acknowledging and amending his faults?

TOMMY.

But what would every body say, if a young gentleman like me, was to go and beg pardon of a farmer's son?

Mr. BARLOW.

They will probably say that you have more sense and gratitude than they expected. However, you are to act as you please;

with the sentiments you still seem to entertain, Harry will certainly be a very unfit companion, and you will do much better to cultivate the new acquaintance you have made.

Mr. Barlow was then going away, but Tommy burst again into tears and begged him not to go; upon which Mr. Barlow said, I do not want to leave you, Tommy, but our conversation is now at an end. You have asked my advice, which I have given you freely. I have told you how you ought to act, if you would preserve the esteem of any good or sensible friend, or prevail upon Harry to excuse your past behaviour. But as you do not approve of what I suggested, you must follow your own opinions.

Pray, sir, pray sir, said Tommy sobbing, do not go. I have used Harry Sandford in the most barbarous manner; my father is angry with me; and if you desert me, I shall have no friend left in the world.

Mr. Barlow.

That will be your own fault, and, therefore, you will not deserve to be pitied. Is it not in your own power to preserve all your friends, by an honest confession of your faults? Your father will be pleased, Harry Sandford will heartily forgive you, and I shall retain the same good opinion of your character which I have long had.

Tommy.

And is it really possible, sir, that you should have a good opinion of me, after all I have told you about myself?

Mr. Barlow.

I have always thought you a little vain and careless, I confess; but, at the same time, I imagined you had both good sense and generosity in your character; I depended upon the first to make you see your faults, and upon the second to correct them.

Tommy.

Dear sir, I am very much obliged to you: but you have always been extremely kind and friendly to me.

Mr. Barlow.

And, therefore, I told your father yesterday, who is very much hurt at your quarrel with Harry, that though a sudden passion

passion might have transported you too far, yet, when you came to consider the matter coolly, you would perceive your faults and acknowledge them: were you not to behave in this manner, I owned I could say nothing in your favour. And I was very much confirmed in this opinion, when I saw the courage you exerted in the rescue of Harry's lamb, and the compassion you felt for the poor highlander. A boy, said I, who has so many excellent dispositions, can never persist in bad behaviour. He may do wrong by accident, but he will be ashamed of his errors, and endeavour to repair them by a frank and generous acknowledgment. This has always been the conduct of really great and elevated minds; while mean and groveling ones alone imagine that it is necessary to persist in faults they have once committed.

TOMMY.

Oh, sir!—I will go directly, and intreat Harry to forgive me; I am convinced that all you say is right.—But will you not go with me? Do, pray, sir, be so good.—

Mr. BARLOW.

Gently, gently, my good friend; you are always for doing every thing in an instant.

I am very glad you have taken a refolution which will do you fo much credit, and give fo much fatisfaction to your own mind: but before you execute it, I think it will be neceffary to fpeak to your father and mother upon the fubject, and, in the mean time, I will go and pay a vifit to farmer Sandford, and bring you an account of Harry.

TOMMY.

Do, fir, be fo good; and tell Harry, if you pleafe, that there is nothing I defire fo much as to fee him; and that nothing fhall ever make me behave ill again. I have heard too, fir, that there was a poor black, that came begging to us, who faved Harry from the bull; if I could but find him out, I would be good to him as long as I live.

Mr. Barlow commended Tommy very much for difpofitions fo full of gratitude and goodnefs, and taking leave of him, went to communicate the converfation he had juft had to Mr. Merton. That gentleman felt the fincereft pleafure at the account, and entreated Mr. Barlow to go directly to prepare Harry to receive his fon. That little boy, added he, has the nobleft mind

mind that ever adorned an human being; nor shall I ever be happy till I see my son acknowledging all his faults, and intreating forgiveness: for, with the virtues that I have discovered in his soul, he appears to me a more eligible friend and companion than noblemen or princes.

Mr. Barlow, therefore, set out on foot, though Mr. Merton would have sent his carriage and servants to attend him, and soon arrived at Mr. Sandford's farm. It was a pleasant spot, situated upon the gentle declivity of an hill, at the foot of which winded along a swift and clear little stream. The house itself was small, but warm and convenient, furnished with the greatest simplicity, but managed with perfect neatness. 'As Mr. Barlow approached, he saw the owner himself guiding a plough through one of his own fields, and Harry, who had now resumed the farmer, directed the horses. But when he saw Mr. Barlow coming across the field, he stopt his team, and letting fall his whip, sprang forward to meet him with all the unaffected eagerness of joy. As soon as Harry had saluted Mr. Barlow, and inquired after his health, he asked him with the greatest kindness after Tommy; for I fancy, sir, said he, by the way

way which I see you come, you have been at Mr. Merton's house. Indeed I have, replied Mr. Barlow, but I am very sorry to find that Tommy and you are not upon as good terms as you formerly were.

HARRY.

Indeed, sir, I am very sorry for it myself. But I do not know that I have given master Merton any reason to change his sentiments about me: and though I do not think he has treated me as well as he ought to do, I have the greatest desire to hear that he is well.

Mr. BARLOW.

That you might have known yourself, had you not left Mr. Merton's house so suddenly, without taking leave of any one, even your friend Mr. Merton, who has always treated you with so much kindness.

HARRY.

Indeed, sir, I shall be very unhappy if you think I have done wrong; but be so good as to tell me how I could have acted otherwise. I am very sorry to appear to accuse master Merton, neither do I bear any resentment against him for what he has done, but since you speak to me upon
the

the subject, I shall he obliged to tell the truth.

Mr. BARLOW.

Well, Harry, let me hear it. You know I shall be the last person to condemn you if you do not deserve it.

HARRY.

I know your constant kindness to me, sir, and I always confide in it: however, I am not sensible now that I am in fault. You know, sir, that it was with great unwillingness I went to Mr. Merton's, for I thought there would be fine gentlemen and ladies there that would ridicule my dress and manners: and though master Merton has been always very friendly in his behaviour towards me, I could not help thinking that he might grow ashamed of my company at his own house.

Mr. BARLOW.

Do you wonder at that, Harry, considering the difference there is in your rank and fortune?

HARRY.

No, sir, I cannot say I do, for I generally observe that those who are rich will scarcely

treat

treat the poor with common civility. But, in this particular case, I did not see any reason for it. I never desired master Merton to admit me to his company or invite me to his house, because I knew that I was born and bred in a very inferior station. You were so good as to take me to your house, and there I became acquainted with him; and if I was then much in his company, it was because he seemed to desire it himself, and I always endeavoured to treat him with the greatest respect.

Mr. BARLOW.

That, indeed, is true, Harry; in all your little plays and studies I have never observed any thing but the greatest mildness and good-nature on your part.

HARRY.

I hope, sir, it has never been otherwise. But though I have the greatest affection for master Merton, I never desire to go home with him. What sort of a figure could a poor boy like me make at a gentleman's table, among little master and misses that powder their hair, and wear buckles as big as our horses carry upon their harness? If I attempted to speak, I was always laughed at;

at, or if I did any thing, I was sure to hear something about clowns and rustics! And yet, I think, though they were all gentlemen and ladies, you would not much have approved of their conversation, for it was about nothing but plays, and dress, and trifles of that nature. I never heard one of them mention a single word about saying their prayers, or being dutiful to their parents, or doing any good to the poor.

Mr. BARLOW.

Well, Harry, but if you did not like their conversation, you surely might have borne it with patience for a little while: and then, I heard something about your being quarrelsome.

HARRY.

Oh, sir, I hope not.—I was to be sure once a little passionate, but that I could not help, and I hope you will forgive me. There was a modest, sensible young lady, that was the only person who treated me with any kindness; and a bold, forward, ill-natured boy, affronted her in the grossest manner, only because she took notice of me. Could I help taking her part? Have you not told me too, sir, that every person,

though

though he should avoid quarrels, has a right to defend himself when he is attacked?

Mr. BARLOW.

Well, Harry, I do not much blame you, from the circumstances I have heard of that affair: but why did you leave Mr. Merton's family so abruptly, without speaking to any body, or thanking Mr. Merton himself for the civilities he had shown you? Was that right?

HARRY.

Oh, dear, sir, I have cried about it several times, for I think I must appear very rude and ungrateful to Mr. Merton. But as to master Tommy, I did not leave him while I thought I could be of any use. He treated me, I must say, in a very unworthy manner; he joined with all the other fine little gentlemen in abusing me, only because I endeavoured to persuade them not to go to a bull-baiting; and then at last he struck me. I did not strike him again, because I loved him so much, in spite of all his unkindness; nor did I leave him till I saw he was quite safe in the hands of his own servants. And, then, how could I go back to his house, after what he had done to me?

I did

I did not choose to complain of him to Mr. Merton; and how could I behave to him as I had done before without being guilty of meanness and falsehood? And therefore I thought it better to go home, and desire you to speak to Mr. Merton; and intreat him to forgive my rudeness.

Mr. BARLOW.

Well, Harry, I can inform you that Mr. Merton is perfectly satisfied upon that account. But there is one circumstance you have not mentioned, my little friend, and that is your saving Tommy's life from the fury of the enraged bull.

HARRY.

As to that, sir, I hope I should have done the same for any human creature. But I believe that neither of us would have escaped, if it had not been for the poor courageous black, that came to our assistance.

Mr. BARLOW.

I see, Harry, that you are a boy of a noble and generous spirit, and I highly approve of every thing you have done: but, are you determined to forsake Tommy Merton

Merton for ever, becaufe he has once behaved ill?

HARRY.

I, fir! no, I am fure. But, though I am poor, I do not defire the acquaintance of any body that defpifes me. Let him keep company with his gentlemen and ladies, I am fatisfied with companions in my own ftation. But furely, fir, it is not I that forfake him, but he that has caft me off.

Mr. BARLOW.

But if he is forry for what he has done, and only defires to acknowledge his faults, and obtain your pardon?

HARRY.

Oh, dear, fir! I fhould forget every thing in an inftant. I knew mafter Tommy was always a little paffionate and headftrong; but he is at the fame time generous and good-natured; nor would he, I am fure, have treated me fo ill, if he had not been encouraged to it by the other young gentlemen.

Mr. BARLOW.

Well, Harry, I believe your friend is thoroughly fenfible of his faults, and that you will have little to fear for the future. He is impatient till he sees you and asks your forgiveness

HARRY.

Oh, sir, I should forgive him if he had beaten me an hundred times. But, though I cannot leave the horses now, if you will be so kind to wait a little, I dare say my father will let me go when he leaves off ploughing.

Mr. BARLOW.

No, Harry, there is no occasion for that. Tommy has indeed used you ill, and ought to acknowledge it; otherwise he will not deserve to be trusted again. He will call upon you, and tell you all he feels upon the occasion. In the mean time, I was desired, both by him and Mr. Merton, to enquire after the poor negro that served you so materially and saved you from the bull.

HARRY.

He is at our house, sir; for I invited him home with me; and, when my father heard how well he had behaved, he made him up a little bed over the stable, and gives him victuals every day; and the poor man seems very thankful and industrious, and says he
would

would gladly do any kind of work to earn his subsistence.

Mr. Barlow then took his leave of Harry, and, after having spoken to his father, returned to Mr. Merton. During his absence, Mr. Simmons had arrived there to fetch away his niece: but, when he had heard the story of the highlander, he perfectly recollected his name and character, and was touched with the sincerest compassion for his sufferings. Upon conversing with the poor man, he found that he was extremely well acquainted with agriculture, as well as truly industrious, and therefore instantly proposed to settle him in a small farm of his own, which happened to be vacant. The poor man received this unexpected change in his fortune with tears of joy, and every mark of unaffected gratitude; and Mr. Merton, who never wanted generosity, insisted upon having a share in his establishment. He proposed to supply him with the necessary instruments of agriculture, and a couple of horses, to begin the culture of his land. Just in that moment, Mr. Barlow entered, and, when he had heard, with the sincerest pleasure, the improvement of his circumstances, begged permission to share in so benevolent an action.

action. I have an excellent milch cow, said he, which I can very well spare, whose milk will speedily recruit the strength of these poor children; and I have half a dozen ewes and a ram, which I hope, under Mr. Campbell's management, will soon increase to a numerous flock. The poor highlander seemed almost frantic with such a profusion of unexpected blessings, and said, that he wished nothing more than to pass the remainder of his days in such a generous nation, and to be enabled to show at least the sentiments which such undeserved generosity had excited.

At night, Mr. Merton, who was desirous, by every method, to support the good impressions which had now taken possession of Tommy's mind, proposed that Miss Simmons should favour them with the conclusion of the story which she had begun the night before. That young lady instantly complied, and read them

The Conclusion of the Story of SOPHRON *and*
TIGRANES.

THE venerable Chares continued his narration thus: I passed several months among the Arabians, delighted with the simplicity
of

of their life and the innocence of their manners: and would to heaven, added he, with a sigh, that I had accepted their friendly invitations, and never quitted the silence of their hospitable deserts! How many scenes should I have avoided, which fill these aged eyes with tears, and pierce my soul with horror, as often as I recollect them! I should not have been witness to such a waste of human blood, nor traced the gradual ruin of my country. I should not have seen our towns involved in flames, nor our helpless children the captives of fell barbarians. But it is in vain for human beings to repine at the just decrees of Providence, which have consigned every people to misery and servitude that abandon virtue, and attach themselves to the pursuit of pleasure.

I left Arabia, with an heart penetrated with gratitude and admiration for its virtuous and benevolent inhabitants. They dismissed me with every mark of kindness and hospitality, guided me over their dreary deserts, and, at parting, presented me with one of those beautiful horses, which are the admiration of all the surrounding nations. I will not trouble you with an account of the different countries which I wandered over in search of wisdom and experience. At length I re-

I returned to my native city, determined to pass the rest of my life in obscurity and retirement: for the result of all my observations was, that he is happiest, who passes his time in innocent employments and the observation of nature. I had seen the princes and nobles of the earth repining in the midst of their splendid enjoyments, disgusted with the empty pageantry of their situation, and wishing, in vain, for the humble tranquillity of private life. I had visited many of the principal cities in several countries where I had travelled, but I had uniformly observed, that the miseries and crimes of mankind increased with their numbers. I therefore determined to avoid the general contagion, by fixing my abode in some sequestered spot, at a distance from the passions and pursuits of my fellow-creatures. I collected the remainder of my effects, and with them purchased a little farm and vineyard in a beautiful and solitary spot near the sea. Soon afterwards I married a virtuous young woman, and, in her society, enjoyed for several years as great a degree of tranquillity as generally falls to the lot of man. I did not disdain to exercise with my own hands the different employments of agriculture; for I thought man was dishonoured by that indolence

indolence which renders him a burthen to his fellow-creatures, not by that induſtry which is neceſſary to the ſupport of his ſpecies. I, therefore ſometimes guided the plough with my own hands, ſometimes laboured in a little garden which ſupplied us with excellent fruits and herbs. I tended the cattle, whoſe patient labour enabled us to ſubdue the ſoil, and conſidered myſelf as only repaying part of the obligations I had received. My wife too exerciſed herſelf in domeſtic cares; ſhe milked the ſheep and goats, and chiefly prepared the food of the family. Amid my other employments, I did not entirely forget the ſtudy of philoſophy, which had charmed me ſo much in my early youth. I frequently obſerved, with admiration, the wiſdom and contrivance which were diſplayed in all the productions of nature, and the perfections of all her works. I uſed to walk amid the coolneſs and ſtillneſs of the evening, feeding my mind with pleaſing meditations upon the power and wiſdom which have originally produced and ſtill ſupport this frame of things. I turned my eyes upon the earth, and ſaw it covered with innumerable animals, that ſported upon its ſurface, and found each according to his nature, ſubſiſtence adapted

H 2 to

to his wants. I faw the air and water themfelves teeming with life, and peopled with innumerable fwarms of infects. I faw, that throughout the whole extent of the creation, as far as I was capable of obferving it, nothing was wafte or defolate; every thing was replete with life, and adapted to fupport it. Thefe reflections continually excited in my mind new gratitude and veneration for that myfterious Being, whofe goodnefs prefides over fuch an infinite variety of beings. I endeavoured to elevate my thoughts to contemplate his nature and qualities; I, however, found my faculties too bounded to comprehend the infinite perfections of his nature. I therefore contented myfelf with imperfectly tracing him in his works, and adoring him as the common friend and parent of all his creatures.

Nor did I confine myfelf to thefe fpeculations, however fublime and confolatory to the human heart. Deftined as we are to inhabit this globe of earth, it is our intereft to be acquainted with its nature and the properties of its productions. For this reafon, I particularly examined all the vegetables which are capable of becoming the food of man, or of the various animals which contribute

tribute to his support; I studied their qualities, the soil in which they delighted, the the improvements which might be made in every species. I sometimes wandered among the neighbouring mountains, and wherever the fall of rocks, or the repeated violence of torrents, had borne away the soil, I considered, with silent admiration, the various substances which we call by the common name of earth. These I used to collect and mingle with the mould of my own garden, by which means I frequently made useful discoveries in fertilizing the soil, and increasing the quantity of food.

I also considered the qualities of the air which surrounds and sustains all living animals. I particularly remarked the noxious or salutary effects it is able to produce upon their constitutions, and, by these means, was frequently enabled to give useful counsels to all the neighbourhood. A large tract of ground had been formerly deluged by the sea, and the waters, finding no convenient vent, spread themselves all around, and converted a large extent of soil into a filthy marsh. Every year, when the heat of summer prevailed, the atmosphere was filled with putrid exhalations, which produced fevers and pestilential disorders among the inhabitants.

bitants. Touched with compaffion for the evils which they endured, I perfuaded them to undertake the tafk of draining the foil, and letting off the fuperfluous waters. This I inftructed them to do with fuch fuccefs, that, in a fhort time, an unwholfome defert became covered with the moft luxuriant harvefts, and was deprived of all its noxious influence. By thus rendering my fervices ufeful to my fellow-creatures, I received the pureft reward which can attend the increafe of knowledge, the confcioufnefs of performing my duty, and humbly imitating that Being, whofe goodnefs is as general and unbounded as his power.

Amid thefe tranquil and innocent employments, my life flowed gently away like a clear and even ftream; I was a ftranger to avarice, to ambition, and to all the cares which agitate the bulk of mortals. Alternate labour and ftudy preferved the vigour both of body and mind; our wants were few and eafily gratified; we chiefly fubfifted upon the liberal returns of the earth, and feldom polluted our table with the bodies of flaughtered animals. One only child, the unfortunate girl who owes her prefervation to the courage of this young man, was granted to our prayers. But in her we found enough to
exercife

exercife all the affections of our minds. We hung with extacy upon her innocent fmiles, and remarked her opening graces with all the partiality of parental fondnefs. As fhe grew up, her mother inftructed her in all the arts and employments of her fex; while I, who already faw the tempeft gathering, which has fince burft with fuch fatal fury upon my country, thought it neceffary to arm her mind with all the firmnefs which education can beftow. For this reafon, I endeavoured to give both to her mind and body a degree of vigour, which is feldom found in the female fex. As foon as fhe was fufficiently advanced in ftrength to be capable of the lighter labours of hufbandry and gardening, I employed her as my conftant companion. Selene, for that was her name, foon acquired a dexterity in all thefe ruftic employments, which I confidered with equal pleafure and admiration. If women are in general feeble both in body and mind, it arifes lefs from nature than from education. We encourage a vicious indolence and inactivity, which we falfely call delicacy; inftead of hardening their minds by the feverer principles of reafon and philofophy, we breed them to ufelefs arts, which terminate in vanity and fenfuality. In moft of the countries which I had vifited, they are taught nothing of an higher nature than a few modulations of the voice, or ufelefs poftures of the body; their time is confumed in floth or trifles, and trifles become the only purfuits capable of interefting them. We feem to forget, that it is upon the qualities of the female fex, that our own domeftic comforts, and the education of our children muft depend. And what are the comforts or the education which a race of beings, corrupted from their infancy, and unacquainted with all the duties of life, are fitted to beftow? To touch a mufical inftrument with ufelefs fkill, to exhibit their natural or affected graces to the eyes of indolent and debauched young men, to diffipate their hufband's patrimony in riotous and unneceffary expences, thefe are the only arts cultivated by women in moft of the polifhed nations I had feen. And the confequences are uniformly fuch as may be expected to proceed from fuch polluted fources, private mifery, and public fervitude.

But Selene's education was regulated by different views, and conducted upon feverer principles; if that can be called feverity, which opens the mind to a fenfe of moral and religious duties, and moft effectually arms it againft the inevitable evils of life.

With

With the rising sun she left her bed, and accompanied me to the garden or the vineyard. Her little hands were employed in shortening the luxurious shoots of fruitful trees, that supplied our table with wholesome and delicious fruits; or in supporting the branches of such as sunk beneath their load. Sometimes she collected water from a clear and constant rill that rolled along the valley, and recruited the force of plants that were exhausted by the sun. With what delight did I view her innocent chearfulness and assiduity! With what pleasure did she receive the praises which I gave to her skill and industry; or hear the lessons of wisdom and the examples of virtuous women, which I used to read her at evening, out of the writings of celebrated philosophers which I had collected in my travels!

But such a life was too unchecquered with misfortune to last. The first stroke which attacked and almost destroyed my hopes of good, was the untimely loss of my dear and virtuous wife. The pestilential heats of autumn overpowered her tender frame, and raised a consuming fever in her veins. For some time she struggled against the disease, but at length her pure and innocent spirit forsook

forsook this earth for ever, and left me, comfortless and forlorn, to mourn her loss.

I will not, my worthy hosts, attempt to describe the inexpressible distress which seized my soul at seeing myself thus deserted. There are some philosophers that aspire to triumph over human feelings; and consider all tender affections as disgraceful weaknesses: for my part, I have never pretended to that degree of insensibility. I have, indeed, opposed as criminal, that habitual acquiescence in sorrow which renders us unfit for the discharge of our duties; but while I have endeavoured to act, I have never blushed at feeling, like a man. Even now that time has mitigated the keenness of the smart, I feel the habitual anguish of an incurable wound. But let me rather hasten to relate the few remaining events of an uniform, unvaried life, than detain you with an useless repetition of my sorrows.

Scarcely had time afforded me a feeble comfort, when the recollection of past misfortunes was almost extinguished by the new ones which overwhelmed my country. The fertile plains of Syria abounded in all the necessaries and conveniencies of life. The vine seemed to grow spontaneously in every valley,

valley, and offer its luxuriant produce to every hand. The induſtrious inſect which ſpins the wonderful ſubſtance called ſilk out of its bowels, though lately introduced into that part of Aſia, ſeemed to receive new vigour from the mildneſs of the climate. Corn and oil, the nobleſt fruits, and the moſt ſalubrious herbs, were found in the garden of every peaſant; and the herds of cattle and horſes, which wandered over our luxuriant paſtures, equalled or ſurpaſſed all I had obſerved in other countries. But this profuſion of bleſſings, inſtead of being attended with any beneficial effects, produced nothing but a fooliſh taſte for frivolous employment and ſenſuality. Feaſts, and dances, and muſic, the tricks of players, and exhibitions of buffoons, were more attended to than all the ſerious and important cares of life. Every young man was a critic in the ſcience of adjuſting the folds of his robe, or of giving a ſtudied negligence to his hair; every young woman was inſtructed in every art that ſerves to conſume time or endanger modeſty. Repeat to them an idle tale, the tricks of a gameſter, or the adventures of a ſinging girl, and every audience liſtened with mute attention to the wonderful narration; but tell them of the ſituation of their country, the

wretched

wretched state of their civil and military discipline, or of the numerous and warlike tribes of barbarians which surround them, and every auditor would steal away in silence, and leave the uninteresting theme.

In such a state of things it was not long to be expected that my countrymen would be permitted to hold the riches they abused, and wanted firmness to defend. A warlike tribe of barbarians burst forth from the northern mountains of Asia, and spread themselves over our fertile plains, which they laid waste like a consuming tempest. After a few ineffectual skirmishes, which only served to expose their weakness to the contempt of their enemies, they yielded without opposition to the invader; in this, indeed, more wise than to irritate him by a fruitless resistance: and thus, in a few weeks, the leader of an obscure tribe of barbarians saw himself become a powerful monarch, and possessor of one of the richest provinces of Asia.

I was sitting one evening at the door of my cottage, gazing upon the fading glory of the setting sun, when a man of a majestic appearance, but with something ferocious in his look, attended by several others, past by. As he approached my little garden
he

he seemed to view it with satisfaction, and to unbend the habitual sternness of his look: I asked him if he would enter in and taste the fruits with his companions. He accepted my offer; and, entering into a shady arbour, I brought him the most palatable fruits I could find, with milk and other rustic fare, such as my farm afforded. He seemed pleased with his entertainment, and when he was departing, thanked me with great affability, and bade me ask a favour in return; which, added he, with a certain degree of conscious pride, you can scarcely make too great either for my gratitude or power. If, answerered I, for I began to suspect that it was Arsaces, the leader of these barbarians, your power is indeed equal to every boon, give peace and liberty to my country. The first, said he, I have already given; and, as to the second, it is impossible; their vices and effeminacy render them incapable of enjoying it. Men that have neither virtue, temperance, nor valour, can never want a master; even though Arsaces were to withdraw his conquering troops. But ask again, added he, something for thyself, and let the favour be worthy me to bestow. Heaven, answered I, with a smile, has already given every thing that

that I can want, when it gave the earth fertility, and me the power to labour. All, therefore, that I requeſt, O mighty conqueror, is, that you will pleaſe to order your men to ſtep aſide from the newly cultivated ground, and not deſtroy my vegetables. By heavens, ſaid Arſaces, turning to his companions, there is ſomething elevated in the tranquillity and compoſure of this man's mind; and, were I not Arſaces, I ſhould be with pleaſure, Chares. He then departed, but ordered me to attend him the next day at the camp, and gave ſtrict orders that none of the ſoldiers ſhould moleſt me, or injure my humble reſidence.

I attended the great Arſaces at the time he had appointed, and traverſed the encampment of his troops with admiration and regret. This people was a tribe of that mighty empire which is called Scythia, whoſe inhabitants have ſo often iſſued from their deſerts for the conqueſt and deſtruction of their neighbours. This country extends to an unknown length behind the moſt fertile diſtricts of Europe and Aſia. The climate is cold in winter, and the earth for ſeveral months covered with ſnow; but in ſummer it feels the enlivening influence of the ſun, and for that reaſon is poſſeſſed of an amazing degree of fertility. But, as the inhabitants live remote from the sea, and poffefs few navigable rivers, they are little acquainted with agriculture or the arts of life. Inftead of trufting to the increafe of their fields for food, they raife prodigious herds of cattle and horfes in the luxuriant paftures, which every where abound. The Scythians, like the Arabians, wander over thefe immenfe fpaces without a fixed or permanent refidence. By the fide of lakes and rivers, where the verdure is more conftant, and the vegetation ftronger, they generally encamp, until the heats of the fummer compel them to afcend the mountains and feek a cooler refidence. Their houfes are compofed of flender poles covered with fkins or a coarfe cloth, and therefore eafily erected, or taken down and ftowed in waggons, for the convenience of tranfporting them in their marches. Their diet is anfwerable to the poverty of their habitations. They milk their herds, and above all, their mares, and preferve the produce in large bottles for months together. This four and homely mefs is to them the greateft dainty, and compofes the chief of their nourifhment. To this they add the flefh of their cattle and horfes, which they kill when afflicted

afflicted with disease, but rarely in health. This is the simple and uniform life of all the Scythians; but this simplicity renders them formidable to all their neighbours, and irresistible in war. Unsoftened by ease or luxury, unacquainted with the artificial wants of life, these nations pass their lives in manly exercises and rustic employments. But horsemanship is the greatest pride and passion of their souls: nor is there an individual who does not at least possess several of these noble animals. These, though small in size, are admirably adapted for the fatigues of war and the chace, and endowed with incomparable swiftness. As to the Scythians themselves, they excel all other nations, unless it be the Arabs, in their courage and address in riding. Without a saddle, or even a bridle, their young men will vault upon an unbacked courser, and keep their seats in spite of all his violent efforts, till they have rendered him tame and obedient to their will. In their military expeditions they neither regard the obstacles of nature, nor the inclemencies of the season, and their horses are accustomed to traverse rocks and mountains with a facility that is incredible. If they reach a river, instead of waiting for the tedious assistance of

boats

boats and bridges, the warrior divests himself of his cloaths and arms, which he places in a bundle upon his horse's back, and then, plunging into the stream, conducts him over by the bridle. Even in the midst of winter, when the hatred of other nations gives way to the inclemencies of the season, the Scythian follows his military labours; and rejoices to see the earth thick covered with frost and snow, because it affords him a solid path to his excursions. Neither the severest cold, nor the most violent storms, can check his ardour. Wrapt up in the thick furs of animals, the patient horseman pursues his march, while all his food for weeks together is comprized in a little bag of seeds or corn. Javelins, and bows and arrows, are the arms which this people are taught from their infancy to use with surprizing dexterity: and, no less dangerous when they fly than when they charge the enemy in front, they are accustomed to shoot with an unerring aim at their pursuers, and turn the fortune of the battle.

Such men are scarcely to be conquered by the efforts of the most powerful nations or sovereigns; and, therefore, the proudest conquerors of the world have failed in their attempts to subdue them. Darius, one of the

the greateſt kings which the vaſt empire of Perſia ever obeyed, once attempted the exploit, and had nearly periſhed in the attempt.

He advanced with a powerful army, but ill prepared for ſuch an expedition, into the Scythian waſtes. The inhabitants, well acquainted with the moſt effectual methods of defence, tranſported their families and herds into the interior parts of the country; and, mounting their fleeteſt horſes, ſeemed to fly before the monarch. Infatuated with pride and confidence he purſued the chace for ſeveral days, until he found himſelf in the midſt of ſolitary deſerts, totally deſtitute of all that human wants require, where his army could neither advance nor retire, without equal danger of periſhing by thirſt and famine. When they ſaw him thus involved, the Scythian horſemen began to check their ſpeed; inſtead of flying, as uſual, they hemmed him in on every ſide, and harraſſed the army with continual attacks. It was then they ſent a preſent to the Perſian king; whoſe myſterious meaning increaſed the terrors of his ſituation. A Scythian, mounted upon a fiery ſteed, entered the camp at full ſpeed, and, regardleſs of danger or oppoſition, penetrated even to the

royal

royal tent, where Darius was holding a council with his nobles. While they were all amazed at this extraordinary boldness, the man leaped lightly from his horse, and, placing a little bundle upon the ground, vaulted up again with inconceivable agility, and retired with the same happy expedition. The curiosity of the monarch made him instantly order the packet to be examined, which contained only a mouse, a bird, a fish, and a bundle of arrows. Silence and astonishment for some time seized the assembly; till, at length, the king observed, that he thought the present which the Scythians had sent could signify nothing but their submission to his arms. The mouse, said he, must represent the earth, because he resides in holes which he digs in the soil; the fish inhabits the waters, and the bird resides in air; by sending me, therefore, all these various animals, they mean to signify that they resign their air, their waters, and their earth, to my dominion: nor is the bundle of arrows more difficult to be explained: these constitute their principal defence, and, by sending them to an enemy, they can intimate nothing but terror and submission.

All

All who were prefent applauded this difcourfe of the monarch, excepting Gobrias, a man of fingular wifdom and experience, who, when he was preffed to declare his fentiments, fpoke to him thus: It is with the greateft reluctance, O king, that I find myfelf compelled to explain thefe prefents of our enemies in a very different manner. That the Scythians, who have hitherto fhewn no marks either of fear or fubmiffion, fhould, on a fudden, feel fo great a terror of the Perfian arms, I cannot eafily believe: more efpecially when I confider, that our army is very much reduced by the diftrefs it has fuffered, and environed on every fide by the enemy, whofe boldnefs vifibly increafes with our neceffities. What, therefore, I fhould infer from this extraordinary prefent is this; they intimate that, unlefs, like the moufe, you can dig your paffage through the earth, or fkim the air like the bird, or glide through waters with the fifh, you fhall certainly perifh by the Scythian arrows.

Such was the fentiment of Gobrias, and all the affembly was ftruck with the evident truth of his interpretation. The king himfelf began to perceive and repent his rafhnefs; inftead of advancing farther into de-
ferts

serts which afforded no subsistence, he resolved to attempt a retreat. This, however, he was not able to effect, without the loss of the greatest part of his troops, who perished by thirst and famine, and the continual attacks of the enemy.

Nor was the expedition of Lysimachus, another powerful king, against this people, less memorable or less unfortunate. His army was defeated, and he himself taken prisoner; but, instead of meeting with that cruelty which we are accustomed to expect from barbarians, he experienced the greatest moderation and humanity from his conquerors. The general of the Scythians invited his captive to a solemn festival, in which he took care to assemble every circumstance of luxury and magnificence which prevails in polished nations. The most exquisite meats were served up to table, and the most generous wines sparkled in golden bowls of the exactest workmanship. Lysimachus was equally delighted with the elegance of the repast and the politeness of the entertainer; but he was extremely surprized, that, instead of sharing in the feast, or even sitting down at table, the Scythian leader reposed in a corner of the tent, upon the bare ground, and satisfied his hunger with

with the moft coarfe and ordinary fare, prepared with all the fimplicity of his country's manners. When the entertainment was finifhed, he afked Lyfimachus which method of life appeared to him the moft agreeable. Lyfimachus could not conceal his preference of the more refined and luxurious dainties, or his diflike of the Scythian diet. If, therefore, replied his generous hoft, you feel fo great a contempt for what this country produces, and fo ftrong a preference for the productions of your own, what but madnefs, O king, can have tempted you to come fo far in order to fubdue men that live in a manner you defpife? Is it not much greater wifdom to be contented with thofe advantages which you prize fo highly, than to expofe them to a certain hazard, for the chance of acquiring what would afford no pleafure or fatisfaction? But let this leffon be fufficient to teach you moderation. A country which produces nothing but iron is not eafily conquered; nor are men, who have been from their infancy inured to every hardfhip, to be vanquifhed by curled and perfumed foldiers, who cannot live without baths, and mufic, and daily feafts. Be contented, therefore, for the futue, to number the Scythians among

among your friends; and rather pray that the gods may keep them in ignorance of the fuperiority of your method of living, left a defire of tafting it fhould tempt them to defert their own country and invade yours. With this difcourfe he generoufly reftored Lyfimachus to liberty, and fuffered him to lead back the fhattered remains of his numerous army.

Such was the nation which had invaded Syria, and eafily triumphed over the efforts of an effeminate and unwarlike people. As I paffed through the camp, I was aftonifhed at the order and regularity which prevailed among thefe barbarians. Some were exercifing their horfes in the mimic reprefentation of a battle; part fled with incredible fpeed, while the reft purfued and darted blunted javelins at their antagonifts. Yet even thofe who fled would frequently turn upon their purfuers, and make them repent their rafhnefs. Some, while their horfes were running in full fpeed, would vault from off their backs to others which accompanied them. Some would gallop by a mark erected for their arrows, and when they had paffed it a confiderable way, turn themfelves round upon their horfes and transfix it with an unerring aim. I faw many

many who vaulted upon their horfes, and placed themfelves between two naked fwords, which would have given them certain death, had they fwerved ever fo little from the juft direction. In another part of the camp, I obferved the children who imitated all the actions of their fathers, and bended little bows adapted to their ftrength, or guided horfes of an inferior ftature along the plain. Their women were indeed inferior to the Syrians in beauty and elegance, but feemed to be of a more robuft conftitution, and more adapted to produce and educate warriors.

I faw no gold, no jewels, no vain and coftly apparel; but all feemed bufy in domeftic cares, preparing the food of their families, or tending upon their infants. At length I reached the royal tent, which fcarcely differed from the reft in its ftructure or fimplicity, and was immediately introduced to the great Arfaces. He received me with a courtefy which had nothing of the barbarian in it, feated me familiarly by his fide, and entered into a long converfation with me upon the laws and manners, and cuftoms of the different nations I had feen. I was furprized at the vigour and penetration which I difcovered in this untutored

tored warrior's mind. Unbiaffed by the mafs of prejudices which we acquire in cities, even from our earlieft childhood, unincumbered by forms and ceremonies which contract the underftanding while they pretend to improve the manners, he feemed to poffefs a certain energy of foul which never miffed the mark. Nature in him had produced the fame effects which ftudy and philofophy do in others. But what amazed me more than all, was to find this Scythian chief as well acquainted with the ftate and confequences of our manners, as if he had paffed his life in Greece or Syria, inftead of the plains and forefts of his own domain. He entertained a rooted contempt for all the arts, which foften the body and mind, under the pretence of adding to the elegancies of life; thefe, he faid, were more efficacious agents to reduce men to flavery, than the fwords and arrows of their enemies.

One day I remembered that fome of our principal men, judging of the mind of their conqueror by their own, brought to him a celebrated dancer; who at that time, engaged the whole attention of our city, and feemed to intereft it much more than the lofs of liberty. This man, who did not

Vol. III.   I   doubt

doubt that he should enchant the soul of a Scythian barbarian, by the same arts which had enraptured his refined audiences at home, exerted himself with an agility that extorted the loudest applause from all the spectators but Arsaces. At length, one of our countrymen took the liberty of asking the monarch, what he thought of this extraordinary performance; I think, replied he, coldly, that it would gain him great credit in a nation of monkies.

Another time, he was present at the exhibitions of a celebrated musician, who was reputed to possess unrivalled skill in playing soft and melting tunes upon the lyre. All the audience seemed to feel the influence of his art, by their inarticulate murmurs of admiration, and the languishing postures of their bodies. When the exhibition was finished, the musician advanced, amid the united plaudits of the audience, as if to receive the just tribute of approbation from Arsaces. But he, with a stern look, said to him, Friend, I permit thee to play every night before the Syrians; but, if thy lyre is ever heard to sound in the presence of my Scythians, I denounce certain death for the offence.

Another

Another time, an officious glutton of our city introduced to him, with great solemnity, two men, whose talents he assured him were unequalled in their different professions. The one, he said, adjusted hair with such dexterity, that he could give an artificial beauty to every countenance; and the other possessed such unrivalled skill in cooking a repast, that even the soberest guest was tempted to commit intemperance. My soldiers, replied Ariaces, are accustomed to adjust their locks with the points of their arrows; nor does our nation consider a bloated paunch and an unwieldy shape, as any accomplishment in warriors; all, therefore, that I can do for these gentlemen, is, to depute one of them to comb my horse's tail, and the other to feed the hogs of the army.

After I had conversed some time with this barbarian chief, who heard me with the greatest attention, the hour of refreshment for the army approached, and I was preparing to retire; but the general stopped me, with a smile, and told me I had already entertained him with the greatest hospitality, and that therefore it was just that I should stay and taste the Scythian food. A bit of dried flesh, which I afterwards found

found was that of an horſe, ſome four, coagulated milk, with an infuſion of certain herbs, thickened with a coarſe kind of flour, were then brought in, and placed upon the ground. I had learned, during my travels in different countries, to diſcard the falſe antipathies which ſo many nations entertain againſt the diet as well as manners of each other. Whatever is adapted to ſupport life is proper for the food of man; habit will reconcile us to every kind of food, and he that can accuſtom himſelf to be the moſt eaſily contented is happieſt, and beſt prepared for performing the duties of life. I therefore placed myſelf by the ſide of Arſaces, and fed without any viſible repugnance upon a diet, which would have excited abhorrence in the minds of all my countrymen. With them it was a work of the greateſt importance to ſettle the formalities of a meal. To contrive a new and poignant ſauce, to combine contrary flavours in a pickle, to ſtimulate the jaded appetite to new exertions, till reaſon and every thing human ſunk under the undigeſted maſs of food, were reckoned the higheſt efforts of genius. Even the magiſtrate did not bluſh to diſplay a greater knowledge of cookery than the laws; the debates of the ſenate itſelf were often ſuſpended

pended by the fear of losing a repast; and many of our generals prided themselves more upon the arrangement of their tables, than the martial evolutions of their troops.

After we had eaten some time, Arsaces asked me what I thought of the Scythian method of living. To speak my sentiments, said I, it is more formidable to your enemies, than agreeable to your friends. He smiled at my sincerity, and I departed; but from this hour he distinguished me with marks of peculiar favour, and admitted me to all his counsels. This envied mark of distinction gave me no other pleasure than as it sometimes enabled me to be useful to my unhappy countrymen, and mitigate the rigour of their conquerors. Indeed, while the great Arsaces lived, his love of justice and order were so great, that even the conquered were safe from all oppression. The peasant pursued his useful labours, unterrified by the march of armies, or unsolicited brought the produce of his fields to a voluntary market. Merchants from all the neighbouring nations crowded to our ports, attracted by the order and justice which were enforced in every part of Arsaces' dominions: and even the vanquished themselves, defended from oppression and protected in their possessions, considered the success of the Scythians rather as a salutary revolution than as a barbarian conquest.

Such was the pleasing prospect of affairs, when an unexpected disease, the consequence of unremitting exertions, put an end to the glorious life of our conqueror; and with him perished all hopes of safety or happiness to the Syrians. His authority alone was capable of restraining so many needy chieftains, so many victorious barbarians: the spirit of rapine and plunder, so long repreft, began now to spread through all the army. Every officer was an independent tyrant, that ruled with despotic authority, and punished as rebellion the least opposition to his will. The fields were now ravaged, the cities plundered, the industrious peasants driven away like herds of cattle, to labour for the caprice of unfeeling masters, or sold in distant regions as slaves. Now it was that the miserable and harassed Syrians began to find, that the riches which they so much esteemed, were but the causes of their ruin, instead of being instrumental to their safety. The poor, accustomed to hardship, have little to fear amid the vicissitudes of life; the brave can always find a refuge in their own valour: but all the bitterness of existence is reserved for those thofe, that have neither courage to defend what they moſt value, nor fortitude to bear the loſs.

To increaſe the weight of our misfortunes, new tribes of barbarians, attracted by the ſucceſs of their countrymen, iſſued from their deſerts, and haſtened to ſhare the ſpoil. But rapine admits not faith or partnerſhip; and it was not long before the vanquiſhed beheld their conquerors animated by implacable rage againſt each other, and ſuffering in turn the violence and cruelties they had inflicted.

At length, one of the principal officers of Arſaces, who is ſaid originally to have deſcended from the mountains which you inhabit, was raiſed to empire by the ſucceſsful efforts of his ſoldiers. He had already attacked and deſtroyed all his competitors, and aſſembled under his banners the remainder of their forces. Tigranes, for thus he is named, poſſeſſes all the courage and activity of Arſaces, but he is deſtitute of his generoſity and clemency. His ambition is vaſt and boundleſs; he graſps at univerſal empire, and rejoices to ſcatter ruin and deſtruction in his way. He has already ſubjected all the maritime cities that derive their origin from Greece, together with the

fertile

fertile plains of Syria. These mountains, inhabited by a bold and hardy race of men, now present a barrier to his enterprizing spirit, and I am assured he already meditates the conquest. His soldiers are drawn together from every part; they swarm like ravening wolves along the fields, and nothing can escape their fury. In vain did I think myself safe in the humble obscurity of my cottage, and the reputed favour of the great Artaces. Yesterday, a lawless band, not contented with destroying my harvest and plundering my little property, seized my daughter and me, and dragged us away in chains. What farther injuries, what farther insults we might have suffered, it is impossible to determine; since Heaven was pleased to effect our deliverance when we had least reason to expect it.

Such was the history of Chares, which Sophron and his family listened to with fixed attention. When he had finished, the father of Sophron again embraced the venerable stranger, and assured him of all the safety which their mountains could bestow. But, added he, if so imminent a danger is near, it behoves us to consult for the general safety; let us assemble all our friends

friends and neighbours, that they may consider whether life is of more confequence than liberty; and, if they determine to retain that freedom which they have received from their anceftors, by what means it may be beft defended. Sophron then immediately went on, and afcending a neighbouring rock, thus fhouted out in a voice which echoed over the neighbouring vallies; Arm, O ye inhabitants of Lebanon, and inftantly meet in council, for a powerful invader is near, and threatens you with death or flavery. This found was inftantly repeated by all who heard it, fo that in a fhort time the intelligence was difperfed to the very confines of the country.

It was not long before a numerous affembly was convened. The aged appeared with all the majeftic dignity of wifdom and experience; their countenances, indeed, indicated the ravages of time, but temperance and exercife had preferved them from the loathfome difeafes which grow on luxury and indolence. They were attended by their fons in all the pride of youth and vigour, who rufhed along in arms, and feemed to breathe deliberate rage and unconquerable oppofition. When they were all affembled upon a fpacious plain, Sophron

phron rofe, and, with a becoming modefty, recited the adventures of the preceding night, and the alarming intelligence he had juft received. He had fcarcely finifhed before a general cry of indignation burft unanimoufly from the whole affembly. When it had a little fubfided, a venerable old man, whofe beard, white as the fnow upon the fummits of the mountains, reached down to his middle, flowly arofe, and leaning upon his ftaff, fpoke thus: Ninety years have I tended my flocks amid thefe mountains, and during all that time I have never feen an human being who was bold enough to propofe to the inhabitants of Lebanon, that they fhould fear death more than infamy, or fubmit to be the vaffals of a tyrant. At this a fecond cry, which feemed to rend the very heavens, was raifed, and farther deliberation judged unneceffary, except upon the moft effectual means of defence. For this purpofe, the aged and more experienced retired to a little diftance to confult. They were not long in their deliberations; it was unanimoufly agreed, that all who were able to bear arms fhould be embodied, and wait for the approach of the enemy within the boundaries of their own mountains. The nature of the country,

try, always rough, and in many parts inaccessible, would afford them, they thought, sufficient advantages even against the more numerous and better disciplined troops of the invader: and, by the common consent of all, Sophron was named the general of his country, and invested with supreme authority for its defence. When these measures had been resolved upon, the assembly dispersed, and Sophron was left alone with Chares. It was then the stranger thus accosted him, with a deep sigh: Did success, O virtuous Sophron, depend entirely upon the justice of the cause, or upon the courage and zeal of its defenders, I should have little doubt concerning the event of the present contest. For, I can truly say, that in all the various countries I have visited, my eyes have never seen a more martial race than I have this day beheld assembled: nor can I doubt that their sentiments correspond to their appearance. All, therefore, that can be effected by patience, activity, and dauntless courage, will be atchieved by your countrymen, in defence of their liberty. But war, unfortunately, is a trade, where long experience frequently confers advantages, which no intrepidity can balance. The troops, which are now approaching, have been for years inured to the practice of slaughter; they join to a courage which defies every danger, a knowledge of every fraud and subtlety which can confound or baffle an adversary. In bodily strength, in numbers, your countrymen are superior; even in courage, and the contempt of danger, they are probably not inferior to their enemies: but such are the fatal effects of military skill and discipline, that I dread the event of a combat with such an army and such a leader.

Alas! answered Sophron, how well do the mature reflections of your wisdom accord with my presaging fears! I know that my countrymen will perform every thing that can be effected by men in their situation; and that thousands will generously sacrifice their lives rather than abandon the cause they have undertaken to defend: yet, when I consider the superior advantages of our enemies, my fears are no less active than your own. This consolation, however, remains, that I shall either see my country victorious, or avoid the miseries which will attend her ruin.

Hear me, then, replied Chares.———The virtues of your friends, my own obligations to yourself, and the desire I feel to oppose
the

the career of mad ambition, conspire to wrest from me a dreadful secret, which I have hitherto buried in my own bosom, and had determined to conceal from the knowledge of mankind. I have already told you that much of my life has been dedicated to the acquisition of knowledge, and the investigation of the laws of nature. Not contented with viewing the appearances of things, as they strike our senses, I have endeavoured to penetrate into the deeper recesses of nature, and to discover those secrets which are concealed from the greater part of mankind. For this purpose, I have tried innumerable experiments concerning the manner in which bodies act upon each other; I have submitted the plants, the stones, the minerals, which surround us, to the violence of all-consuming fires; I have examined their structure, and the different principles which compose them, with the patient labour and perseverance of a long life. In the course of these inquiries, I have made many curious and important discoveries, but one above the rest, which I will now impart, under the promise of eternal and inviolable secrecy. Know, then, that I have found out an easy and expeditious combination of common materials,

the

the effect of which is equal or superior to the most potent and destructive agents in nature. Neither the proudest city can maintain its walls, or the strongest castle its bulwarks, against the irresistible attacks of this extraordinary composition. Increase but the quantity, and the very rocks and mountains will be torn asunder, with a violence that equals that of earthquakes. Whole armies, proud of their triumphs, may be in an instant scattered and destroyed, like the summer's dust before the whirlwind: and, what increases the prodigy, a single man may securely give death to thousands. —This composition I have hitherto concealed, in pity to the miseries of mankind; but, since there appears no other method of preserving the virtuous inhabitants of these mountains from slavery and ruin, I am determined to employ it in their defence. Give orders, therefore, that a certain number of your countrymen provide me with the ingredients that I shall indicate, and expect the amplest success from your own valour, assisted by such powerful auxiliares.

Sophron said every thing to Chares which such an unexpected mark of confidence deserved, and instantly received his orders, and prepared to execute them with the
greatest

greatest alacrity. Chares, mean-while, was indefatigable in the execution of his project, and it was not long before he had prepared a sufficient quantity to provide for the common defence. Tigranes now approached with the rage and confidence of a lion that invades a flock of domestic animals. He had long forgotten all the ties which attach men to the place of their birth, and neither time, nor distance, had been able to extinguish the hatred he had conceived to Sophron. Scarcely did he deign to send an ambassador before his army. He, however, dispatched one with an imperious message, requiring all the inhabitants of Lebanon to submit to his victorious arms, or threatening them with the worst extremities of war. When the ambassador returned, and reported the fixed determination of Sophron and his countrymen, he was inflamed with rage, and ordered his army to advance to the attack. They marched without opposition till they entered the mountainous districts, where all the bravest inhabitants were ranged in arms to meet the invader. Then arose the noise of war and the clang of arms; then man encountered man, and wounds and death were seen on every side. The troops of Tigranes advanced in close array, with

with long protended spears; the inhabitants of Lebanon were lighter armed, and, with invincible courage, endeavoured to break the formidable battalion of their enemies. They rushed with fury upon the dreadful range of weapons, and, even wounded and dying, endeavoured to beat down their points, and open a way to their companions. Sophron was seen conspicuous in every part of the field, encouraging his companions with his voice, and more by his actions. Wherever he turned his steps, he was followed by the bravest youth of his party, and there the efforts and the slaughter were always greatest. Five times, covered with blood and dust, he made a desperate charge upon the troops of Tigranes, and five times did he force his bravest soldiers to give ground. At length, the superiority of discipline and experience began to prevail over the generous, but more unequal efforts of the defenders. The veterans of Tigranes perceived their advantage, and pressed the enemy with redoubled vigour. This was the decisive moment which Chares had foreseen and provided for: in an instant the bands of Lebanon retreat by the orders of Sophron, with a precipitation bordering upon flight. Tigranes, supposing himself

cer-

certain of victory, orders his troops to advance and decide the fortune of the battle; but, while they are rashly preparing to obey, a sudden noise is heard that equals the loudest thunders; the earth itself trembles with a convulsive motion under their feet; then bursts asunder with a violence that nothing can resist. Hundreds are in an instant swallowed up, or dashed against rocks, and miserably destroyed. Meanwhile, all nature seems to be convulsed around; the rocks themselves are torn from their solid base, and with their enormous fragments crush whole bands of miserable wretches beneath. Clouds of smoke obscure the field of battle, and veil the combatants in a dreadful shade; which is, from time to time, dispelled by flashes of destructive fire. Such a succession of horrors daunted even the most brave: scarcely could the troops of Lebanon, who had been prepared to expect some extraordinary interposition, maintain their post, or behold the spectacle of their enemies ruin; but the bands of Tigranes were struck with the wildest consternation, and fled with trembling steps over the field. And now these prodigies were succeeded by an awful interval of quiet; the peals of bursting thunder were

were no longer heard, the lightnings ceased to flash, the mists that darkened the scene were rolled away, and difcovered the various fortunes of the fight. Then the voice of Sophron was heard, exhorting his companions to purfue the fugitives and complete their victory. They rushed forwards like angry lions to the chace; but all refiftance was at an end: and Sophron, who now perceived that the enemy was irretrievably broken, checked the ardour of his men, and intreated them to fpare the vanquifhed. They obeyed his voice, and, after having chaced them beyond the utmoft boundaries of Lebanon, returned in triumph, amid the praifes and acclamations of their joyful families, whom they had preferved from flavery by their valour. They then examined the field of battle, and, collecting all who had any remains of life, they treated them with the greateft humanity, binding up their wounds, and adminiftering to all their neceffities. Among the thickeft dead was found the breathlefs body of Tigranes, miferably fhattered and disfigured, but ftill exhibiting evident marks of paffion and ferocity. Sophron could not behold, without compaffion, the friend of his early years, and the companion of his youthful fports.

Un-

Unhappy man! said he, thou hast, at length, paid the price of thy ungovernable ambition! How much better would it have been to have tended thy flocks upon the mountains, than to have blazed an angry meteor, and set for ever amid the curses of thy country! He then covered the body with a military vest, and ordered it to be honourably burned upon a mighty funeral pile which was prepared for all the dead.

The next day, an immense quantity of spoil was collected that had been abandoned by the troops of Tigranes in their flight. The simple inhabitants of Lebanon, the greater part of whom had never been beyond the limits of their mountains, were astonished at such a display of luxury and magnificence. Already the secret poison of sensuality and avarice began to enflame their hearts, as they gazed on costly hangings, enriched with gold and silver, on Persian carpets, and drinking vessels of the most exquisite workmanship. Already had they begun to differ about the division of these splendid trifles, when Sophorn, who marked the growing mischief, and remembered the fatal effects which Chares had described in his travels, rose, and proposed to his countrymen, that the arms of their conquered
enemies

enemies should be carefully preserved for the public defence, but that all the rest of the spoil should be consumed upon the funeral pile prepared for the dead, lest the simplicity of the inhabitants of Lebanon should be corrupted, and the happy equality and union which had hitherto prevailed among them interrupted. This proposal was instantly applauded by all the older and wiser part of the assembly, who rejoiced in seeing the evils averted which they had so much reason to apprehend: nor did those of a different character dare to express their sentiments, or attempt any open opposition.

From this time, Sophron was universally honoured by all as the most virtuous and valiant of his nation. He passed the rest of his life in peace and tranquillity, contented with the exercise of the same rural employments which had engaged his childhood. Chares, whose virtues and knowledge were equally admirable, was presented, at the public expence, with a small but fertile tract of land, sufficient to supply him with all the comforts of life; this the grateful inhabitants of the mountains continually cultivated for him, as a memorial of the signal assistance he had afforded them; and
here,

here, contented with the enjoyment of security and freedom, he paſſed the remaining part of his life in the contemplation of nature, and the delightful intercourſe of virtuous fiiendſhip.

When Miſs Simmons had finiſhed, Tommy expreſſed his aſtoniſhment at the latter part of the ſtory. Is it poſſible, ſaid he, there can be any thing of ſo extraordinary a nature as to burſt the very rocks aſunder, and deſtroy an army at once?—Have you, then, never heard the exploſion of a gun, or are you ignorant of the deſtructive effects of the powder with which they charge it? ſaid Mr. Barlow.

Tommy.

Yes, ſir; but that is nothing to what Chares did in the ſtory.

Mr. Barlow.

That is only becauſe it is uſed in very inconſiderable portions; but, were you to increaſe the quantity, it would be capable of effecting every thing which you heard Miſs Simmons deſcribe. When nations are at war with each other, it is now univerſally the agent of deſtruction. They have large tubes of iron, called cannons,

into

into which they ram a confiderable quantity of powder, together with a large iron ball, as big as you are able to lift. They then fet fire to the powder, which explodes with fo much violence, that the ball flies out and deftroys, not only every living thing it meets with, but even demolifhes the ftrongeft walls that can be raifed. Sometimes it is buried in confiderable quantities in the earth, and then they contrive to enflame it, and to efcape in time. When the fire communicates with the mafs, it is all enflamed in an inftant, and produces the horrible effects you have heard defcribed. As fuch are the irrefiftible effects of gunpowder, it is no wonder that even a victorious army fhould be ftopped in their progrefs by fuch a dreadful and unexpected event.

TOMMY.

That is true, indeed; and I declare Chares was a very good and fenfible man. Had it not been for him, thefe brave inhabitants of Lebanon muft have been enflaved. I now plainly perceive, that a man may be of much more confequence by improving his mind in various kinds of knowledge, even though he is poor, than by all

the

the finery and magnificence he can acquire. I wish, with all my heart, that Mr. Barlow had been so good as to read this story to the young gentlemen and ladies that were lately here. I think it would have made a great impression upon their minds, and would have prevented their feeling so much contempt for poor Harry, who is better and wiser than them all, though he does not powder his hair, or dress so genteelly.

Tommy, said Mr. Merton, with a kind of contemptuous smile, why should you believe that the hearing of a single story would change the characters of all your late friends, when neither the good instructions you have been so long receiving from Mr. Barlow, nor the intimacy you have had with Harry, were sufficient to restrain your impetuous temper, or prevent you from treating him in the shameful manner you have done?

Tommy appeared very much abashed with his father's rebuke; he hung down his head in silence a considerable time: at length he faintly said; Oh, sir! I have, indeed, acted very ill: I have rendered myself unworthy of the affection of all my best friends. But do not, pray, do not give me up entirely; you shall see how I will

behaved

behave for the future; and if ever I am guilty of the same faults again, I consent that you should abandon me for ever. Saying this, he silently stole out of the room, as if intent upon some extraordinary resolution. His father observed his motions, and, smiling, said to Mr. Barlow, What can this protend? This boy is changeable as a weathercock. Every blast whirls him round and round upon his centre, nor will he ever fix, I fear, in any direction. At least, said Mr. Barlow, you have the greatest reason to rejoice in his present impressions, which are good and estimable. And, I fear, it is the lot of most human beings to exhaust almost every species of error before they fix in truth and virtue.

Tommy now entered the room, but with a remarkable change in his dress and manner. He had combed the powder out of his hair, and demolished the elegance of his curls; he had divested his dress of every appearance of finery, and even his massy and ponderous buckles, so long the delight of his heart, and the wonder of his female friends, were taken from his shoes, and replaced by a pair of the plainest form and appearance. In this habiliment he appeared so totally changed from what he was,
that

that even his mother, who had lately become a little sparing of her observations, could not help exclaiming, What, in the name of wonder, has the boy been doing now! Why, Tommy, I protest you have made yourself a perfect fright, and you look more like a ploughboy than a young gentleman!

Mamma, answered Tommy gravely, I am only now what I ought always to have been. Had I been contented with this dress before, I never should have imitated such a parcel of coxcombs as you have lately had at your house; nor pretended to admire Miss Matilda's music, which, I own, tired me as much as Harry, and had almost set me asleep; nor should I have exposed myself at the play and the ball; and, what is worst of all, I should have avoided all my shameful behaviour to Harry at the bull-baiting. But, from this time, I shall apply myself to the study of nothing but reason and philosophy; and therefore I have bid adieu to dress and finery for ever.

It was with great difficulty that the gentlemen could refrain from laughing at Tommy's harangue, delivered with infinite seriousness and solemnity; they, however, concealed their emotions, and encouraged him to perfevere in fuch a laudable refolution. But, as the night was now pretty far advanced, the whole family retired to bed.

The next morning, early, Tommy arofe and dreffed himfelf with his newly adopted fimplicity; and, as foon as breakfaft was over, intreated Mr. Barlow to accompany him to Harry Sandford's. But he did not forget to take with him the lamb, which he had careffed and fed with conftant affiduity ever fince he had fo valiantly refcued him from his devouring enemy. As they approached the houfe, the firft object which Tommy diftinguifhed was his little friend at fome diftance, who was driving his father's fheep along the common. At this fight, his impetuofity could no longer be reftrained, and, fpringing forward with all his fpeed, he arrived in an inftant, panting, and out of breath, and incapable of fpeaking. Harry, who knew his friend, and plainly perceived the difpofitions with which he approached, met him with open arms; fo that the reconciliation was begun and completed in a moment; and Mr. Barlow, who now arrived witth the lamb, had the pleafure of feeing his little pupils mutually giving and receiving every unaffected mark of the warmeft affection.

Harry

Harry, said Mr. Barlow, I bring you a little friend, who is sincerely penitent for his offences, and comes to own the faults he has committed. That I am indeed, said Tommy, a little recovered and able to speak. But I have behaved so ill, and have been such an ungrateful fellow, that I am afraid Harry will never be able to forgive me. Indeed, indeed, said Harry, there you do me the greatest injustice; for I have already forgotten every thing but your former kindness and affection. And I, answered Tommy, will never forget how ill, how ungratefully I have used you, nor the goodness with which you, now receive me. Tommy then recollected his lamb, and presented it to his friend; while Mr. Barlow told him the story of its rescue, and the heroism exerted in its defence. Harry seemed to receive equal pleasure from the restoration of his favourite, and the affection Tommy had shewn in its preservation, and, taking him by the hand, he led him into a small but neat and convenient house, where he was most cordially welcomed by Harry's family. In a corner of the chimney sat the honest black who had performed so signal a service at the bull-baiting. Alas! said Tommy, there is another instance of my negligence and ingratitude. I now fee that one fault brings on another without end. Then, advancing to the black, he took him kindly by the hand, and thanked him for the prefervation of his life. Little mafter, replied he, you are extremely welcome to all I have done. - I would at any time rifque my own fafety, to preferve one of my fellow-creatures; and, if I have been of any ufe, I have been amply repaid by the kindnefs of this little boy, your friend, and all his worthy family. That is not enough, faid Tommy, and you fhall foon find what it is to oblige a perfon like . . . . . . Here a ftroke of prefumption was juft coming out of Tommy's mouth, but, recollecting himfelf, he added, a perfon like my father. And now he addreffed himfelf to Harry's mother, a venerable decent woman, of a middle age, and his two fifters, plain, modeft, healthy-looking girls, a little older than their brother. All thefe he treated with fo much cordiality and attention, that all the company were delighted with him; fo eafy is it for thofe who poffefs rank and fortune to gain the good-will of their fellow-creatures; and fo inexcufable is that furly pride which renders many of them defervedly odious.

When

When dinner was ready, he sat down with the rest, and as it was the custom here for every body to wait upon himself, Tommy insisted upon their suffering him to conform to the established method. The victuals were not indeed very delicate, but the food was wholesome, clean, and served up hot to table; an advantage which is not always found in elegant apartments. Tommy ate with a considerable appetite, and seemed to enjoy his new situation as much as if he had never experienced any other. After the dinner was removed, he thought he might with propriety gratify the curiosity he felt to converse with the black upon fighting bulls, for nothing had more astonished him than the account he had heard of his courage, and the ease with which he had subdued so terrible an animal. My friend, said he, I suppose in your own country you have been very much used to bull-baitings; otherwise you never would have dared to encounter such a fierce creature; I must confess, though I can tame most animals, I never was more frighted in my life, than when I saw him break loose; and without your assistance, I do not know what would have become of me.

Master,

Master, replied the black, it is not in my own country, that I have learned to manage these animals. There I have been accustomed to several kinds of hunting, much more dangerous than this; and considering, how much you white people despise us blacks, I own I was very much surprized to see so many hundreds of you running away from such an insignificant enemy as a poor tame bull.

Tommy blushed a little at the remembrance of the prejudices he had formerly entertained, concerning blacks and his own superiority; but not choosing now to enter upon the subject, he asked the man where then he had acquired so much dexterity in taming them.

I will tell you, master, replied the black: When I lived a slave among the Spaniards at Buenos Ayres, it used to be a common employment of the people to go into the woods and hunt cattle down for their subsistence. The hunter mounts his fleetest horse, and takes with him a strong cord of a considerable length: when he sees one of the wild kine, which he destines for his prey, he pursues it at full speed, and never fails to overtake it by the superior swiftness of his horse.
While

While he is thus employed, he holds the cord ready, at the end of which a sliding noose is formed;. and when he is at a convenient distance, throws it from him with such a certain hand, that the beast is entangled by one of his legs, after which it is impossible for him to escape.

That you may form the clearer idea of what a man is capable of executing, with courage and addrefs, I will relate a most extraordinary incident to which I was witness, during my residence in that part of the world. A certain man, a native of the country, had committed some offence, for which he was condemned to labour several years in the gallies. He found means to speak to the governor of the town, and besought him to change the nature of his punishment. I have been brought up, said he, a warrior, and fear dishonour, but not death. Instead of consuming my strength and spirits in such an ignominious employment, let me have an opportunity of atchieving something worthy to be beheld, or of perishing like a brave man in the attempt. In a few days a solemn feast is to be celebrated, at which you will not fail to be present, attended by all your people. I will there, in the presence of the whole city, encounter the fiercest bull

bull you can procure. I defire no affiftance but my horfe, no weapons but this cord; yet thus prepared I will meet his fury, and take him by the head, the horns, the feet, as you fhall direct. I will then throw him down, bridle him, faddle him, and vault upon his back; in this fituation, you fhall turn out two more of the fierceft bulls you can find, and I will attack them both, and put them all to death with my dagger, the inftant you fhall command. The governor confented to this brave man's requeft, more from curiofity to fee fo extraordinary a fpectacle, than from the opinion it would be attended with fuccefs. When the appointed day arrived, the inhabitants of all the city affembled, and took their feats in a vaft building which furrounded a confiderable open fpace, deftined for this amazing combat. The brave American then appeared alone on horfeback, armed with nothing but his cord; and, after riding round the place, and faluting the company, he waited intrepidly for his enemy. Prefently, an enormous bull was let loofe, who, as foon as he beheld the man, attacked him with all his fury. The American avoided his fhock with infinite dexterity, and gallopped round the bull, who,

who, in his turn, betook himself to flight. The valiant horseman pursued his flying enemy, and, while he was thus engaged, desired the governor to direct where he would have him seized. He replied, it was a matter of indifference to him; and the American instantly throwing his noose, which he held ready all the time, caught the bull in his flight by one of his hinder legs; then gallopping two or three times round the animal, he so inveloped him in the snare, that, after a few violent efforts to disengage himself, he fell to the earth. He then leaped lightly from his horse, and the animal, who had been perfectly trained up to this kind of combat, stood still and kept the cord extended; while his master advanced to the bull, and put him to death in an instant, by stabbing him with his dagger behind the horns. All the assembly uttered a shout of admiration, but the conqueror told them that what they had seen was nothing, and, disentangling his cord from the slaughtered beast, he composedly mounted his horse, and waited for a new and more formidable enemy. Presently, the gate of the torillo was opened, and a bull, much more furious than the last, rushed out, whom

whom he was ordered to bridle and saddle, according to his engagement.

I proteſt, ſaid Tommy, this is the moſt wonderful ſtory I ever heard. I do not believe all the fine gentlemen I have ever ſeen, put together, would dare to attack ſuch a bull.

Maſter, replied the black, the talents of mankind are various, and nature has, in every country, furniſhed the human ſpecies with all the qualities neceſſary for their preſervation. In this country, and many others which I have ſeen, there are thouſands who live like birds in cages upon the food provided by others, without doing any thing for themſelves. But they ſhould be contented with the happineſs they enjoy, if ſuch a life can be called happineſs, and not deſpiſe their fellow-creatures, without whoſe continual aſſiſtance they could not exiſt an inſtant.

Very true, indeed, anſwered Tommy. You ſeem to me a very honeſt, ſenſible man, though a negro; and, ſince I have given myſelf up to the improvement of my mind, I entertain the ſame opinions. But, let us hear how this brave man ſucceeded in his next attempt.

When

When the champion perceived this second enemy approach, he waited for him with the same intrepidity he had discovered before, and avoided his formidable shock by making his horse wheel nimbly round the bull. When he had thus baffled his fury, and put his enemy to flight, he chaced him some time as he had done the former, till he drove him near to the middle of the enclosed space, where a strong post had been firmly fixed into the ground. As soon as he approached this spot, he threw the unerring noose, and, catching the bull by the horns, entangled him as he had done before, and dragged him with some difficulty to the stake. To this he bound him down so closely that it became impossible for the creature either to resist or stir. Leaping then from his horse, who remained immoveable as before, he took a saddle, which had been left there on purpose, and girded it firmly upon the back of the bull; through his nostrils he thrust an iron ring, to which was fixed a cord which he brought over his neck as a bridle; and then, arming his hand with a short pike, he nimbly vaulted upon the back of this new and terrible courser.

The creature all this time did not cease to

to bellow with every expreſſion of rage, which had not the leaſt effect upon the mind of this valiant man. On the contrary, coolly taking a knife, he cut the cord which bound him to the ſtake, and reſtored him to perfect liberty. The creature, thus diſengaged, exerted every effort of ſtrength and fury to throw his rider, who kept his ſeat undaunted in ſpite of all his violent agitations. The gates of the torillo were then thrown open, and two other furious bulls ruſhed out, and ſeemed ready to attack the man: but, the inſtant they perceived the manner in which he was mounted, their rage gave way to terror, and they fled precipitately away. The other bull followed his companions, and bore his rider ſeveral times round the amphitheatre in this extraordinary chace. This ſpectacle had already laſted ſome time, to the admiration of all preſent, when the governor ordered the man to complete the buſineſs by putting all the bulls to death. He, inſtantly drawing his knife, plunged it behind the horns of the bull on which he rode, who immediately dropped down dead, while the conqueror, diſengaging himſelf as he fell, ſtood upright by the ſlaughtered animal. He then mounted his horſe again, who

who had been placed in safety at some little distance, and pursuing the chace as before, with his fatal noose, dispatched both the surviving animals without the least difficulty.

Tommy expressed the greatest admiration at this recital; and now, as the evening began to advance, Mr. Barlow invited him to return. But Tommy, instead of complying, took him by the hand, thanked him for all his kindness and attention, but declared his resolution of staying some time with his friend Harry. The more I consider my own behaviour, said he, the more I feel myself ashamed of my folly and ingratitude. But you have taught me, my dear sir, that all I have in my power is to acknowledge them, which I most willingly do before all this good family, and intreat Harry to think that the impressions I now feel are such as I shall never forget. Harry embraced his friend, and assured him once more of his being perfectly reconciled; and all the family stood mute with admiration at the condescension of the young gentleman, who was not ashamed of acknowledging his faults even to his inferiors.

Mr. Barlow approved of Tommy's design, and took upon him to answer for the con-

consent of Mr. Merton to his staying some time with Harry; then, taking his leave of all the company, he departed.

But Tommy began now to enter upon a course of life which was very little consistent with his former habits. He supped with great chearfulness, and even found himself happy with the rustic fare which was set before him, accompanied as it was with unaffected civility and an hearty welcome. He went to bed early and slept very sound all night; however, when Harry came to call him the next morning at five, as he had made him promise to do, he found a considerable difficulty in rouzing himself at the summons. Conscious pride, however, and the newly-acquired dignity of his character, supported him; he recollected that he should disgrace himself in the eyes of his father, of Mr. Barlow, and of all the family with which he now was, if he appeared incapable of acting up to his own declarations: he therefore made a noble effort, leaped out of bed, dressed himself, and followed Harry. Not contented with this, he accompanied him in all his rustic employments, and, as no kind of country exercise was entirely new to him since his residence with Mr. Barlow, he acquitted
himself

himself with a degree of dexterity which gained him new commendations.

Thus did he pass the first day of his visit, with some little difficulty indeed, but without deviating from his resolution. The second, he found his change of life infinitely more tolerable; and, in a very little space of time, he was almost reconciled to his new situation. The additional exercise he used improved his health and strength, and added so considerably to his appetite, that he began to think the table of farmer Sandford exceeded all he had ever tried before.

By thus practising the common useful occupations of life, he began to feel a more tender interest in the common concerns of his fellow-creatures. He now found, from his own experience, that Mr. Barlow had not deceived him in the various representations he had made of the utility of the lower classes, and consequently of the humanity which is due to them when they discharge their duty. Nor did that gentleman abandon his little friend in this important trial. He visited him frequently; pointed out every thing that was curious or interesting about the farm, and encouraged him to persevere by his praises. You are now,

now, said Mr. Barlow, one day, beginning to practise those virtues which have rendered the great men of other times so justly famous. It is not by sloth, nor finery, nor the mean indulgence of our appetites, that greatness of character, or even reputation, is to be acquired. He that would excel others in virtue or knowledge, must first excel them in temperance and application. You cannot imagine that men fit to command an army, or to give laws to a state, were ever formed by an idle and effeminate education. When the Roman people, oppressed by their enemies, were looking out for a leader able to defend them, and change the fortune of the war, where did they seek for this extraordinary man? It was neither at banquets, nor in splendid palaces, nor amid the gay, the elegant, or the dissipated; they turned their steps towards a poor and solitary cottage, such as the meanest of your late companions would consider with contempt; there they found Cincinnatus, whose virtues and abilities were allowed to excel all the rest of his citizens, turning up the soil with a pair of oxen, and holding the plough himself. This great man had been inured to arms and the management of public affairs, even from
his

his infancy; he had repeatedly led the Roman legions to victory; yet in the hour of peace, or when his country did not require his services, he deemed no employment more honourable than to labour for his own subsistence.

What would all your late friends have said, to see the greatest men in England, and the bravest officers of the army, crowding round the house of one of those obscure farmers you have been accustomed to despise, and intreating him, in the most respectful language, to leave his fields, and accept of the highest dignity in the government or army? Yet this was actually the state of things at Rome, and it was characters like these, with all the train of severe and rugged virtues, that elevated that people above all the other nations of the world.—And tell me, my little friend, since chance, not merit, too frequently allots the situation in which men are to act, had you rather, in an high station, appear to all mankind unworthy of the advantages you enjoy, or, in a low one, seem equal to the most exalted employments by your virtues and abilities?

Such were the conversations which Mr. Barlow frequently held with Tommy, and which

which never failed to infpire him with new
refolution to perfevere. Nor could he help
being frequently affected by the comparifon
of Harry's behaviour with his own. No
cloud feemed ever to fhade the features of his
friend, or alter the uniform fweetnefs of his
temper. Even the repeated provocations he
had received were either totally obliterated,
or had made no difagreeable impreffions.
After difcharging the neceffary duties of
the day, he gave up the reft of his time to
the amufement of Tommy, with fo much
zeal and affection, that he could not avoid
loving him a thoufand times better than
before.

During the evening he frequently con-
verfed with the honeft negro concerning
the moft remarkable circumftances of the
country where he was born. One night that
he feemed peculiarly inquifitive, the black
gave him the following account of himfelf.

I was born, faid he, in the neighbourhood
of the river Gambia in Africa. In this
country people are aftonifhed at my colour,
and ftart at the fight of a black man, as if
he did not belong to their fpecies: but
there, every body refembles me, and when
the firft white men landed upon our coaft, we
were as much furprized with their appearances

ances as you can be with ours. In some parts of the world I have seen men of a yellow hue, in others of a copper colour, and all have the foolish vanity to despise their fellow-creatures as infinitely inferior to themselves. There indeed they entertain these conceits from ignorance; but in this country, where the natives pretend to superior reason, I have often wondered they could be influenced by such a prejudice. Is a black horse thought to be inferior to a white one, in speed, or strength, or courage? Is a white cow thought to give more milk, or a white dog to have an acuter scent in pursuing the game? On the contrary, I have generally found, in almost every country, that a pale colour in animals is considered as a mark of weakness and inferiority. Why then should a certain race of men imagine themselves superior to the rest, for the very circumstance they despise in other animals?

But in the country where I was born, it is not only man that differs from what we see here, but every other circumstance. Here, for a considerable part of the year, you are chilled by frosts and snows, and scarcely behold the presence of the sun during that gloomy season that is called the winter.

With

With us the sun is always present, pouring out light and heat, and scorching us with his fiercest beams. In my country we know no difference in the length of nights and days: all are of equal length throughout the year, and present not that continual variety which you see here. We have neither ice, nor frost, nor snow; the trees never lose their leaves, and we have fruits in every season of the year. During several months, indeed, we are scorched by unremitting heats, which parch the ground, dry up the rivers, and afflict both men and animals with intolerable thirst. In that season, you may behold lions, tygers, elephants, and a variety of other ferocious animals, driven from their dark abodes in the midst of impenetrable forests, down to the lower grounds and the side of rivers. Every night we hear their savage yells, their cries of rage, and think ourselves scarcely safe in our cottages. In this country you have reduced all other animals to subjection, and have nothing to fear except from each other. You even shelter yourselves from the injuries of the weather in mansions that seem calculated to last for ever, in impenetrable houses of brick or stone, that would have scarcely any thing to fear from the whole animal creation;

creation; but, with us, a few reeds twisted together, and perhaps daubed over with slime or mud, compose the whole of our dwellings. Yet there the innocent negro would sleep as happy and contented as you do in your palaces, provided you did not drag him by fraud and violence away, and force him to endure all the excesses of your cruelty.

It was in one of these cottages that I first remember any thing of myself. A few stakes set in the ground, and interwoven with dry reeds, covered at top with the spreading leaves of the palm, composed our dwelling. Our furniture consisted of three or four earthen pipkins, in which our food was dressed; a few mats woven with a silky kind of grass to serve as beds; the instruments with which my mother turned the ground, and the javelin, arrows, and lines, which my father used in fishing or the chace. In this country, and many others where I have been, I observe that nobody thinks himself happy till he has got together a thousand things which he does not want, and can never use; you live in houses so big, that they are fit to contain an army; you cover yourselves with superfluous clothes, that restrain all the motions of your bodies:
when

when you want to eat, you muſt have meat enough ſerved up to nouriſh a whole village; yet I have ſeen poor famiſhed wretches ſtarving at your gate, while the maſter had before him at leaſt an hundred times as much as he could conſume. We negroes, whom you treat as ſavages, have different manners and different opinions. The firſt thing that I can remember of myſelf was the running naked about ſuch a cottage as I have deſcribed, with four of my little brothers and ſiſters. I have obſerved your children here with aſtoniſhment: as ſoon as they are born, it ſeems to be the buſineſs of all about them, to render them weak, helpleſs, and unable to uſe any of their limbs. The little negro, on the contrary, is ſcarcely born before he learns to crawl about upon the ground. Unreſtrained by bandages or ligatures, he comes as ſoon and as eaſily to the perfect uſe of all his organs as any of the beaſts which ſurround him. Before your children here are taught to venture themſelves upon their feet, he has the perfect uſe of his, and can follow his mother in her daily labours.

This I remember was my own caſe. Sometimes I uſed to go with my mother to the field, where all the women of the village

were

were assembled to plant rice for their subsistence. The joyful songs which they used to sing, amid their toils, delighted my infant ear; and when their daily task was done, they danced together under the shade of spreading palms. In this manner did they raise he simple food, which was sufficient for themselves and their children; yams, a root resembling your potatoe, Indian corn, and, above all, rice; to this were added the fruits which nature spontaneously produced in our woods, and the produce of the chace and fishing. Yet with this we are as much contented as you are with all your splendid tables, and enjoy a greater share of health and strength. As soon as the fiery heat of the sun declined, you might behold the master of every cottage reposing before his own door, and feasting upon his mess of roots or fruits, with all his family around. If a traveller or stranger happened to come from a distant country, he was welcome to enter into every house and share the provisions of the family. No door was barred against his entrance, no surly servant insulted him for his poverty; he entered wherever he pleased, sat himself down with the family, and then pursued his journey, or reposed himself in quiet till the next morning.

morning. In each of our towns there is generally a large building, where the elder part of the fociety are accuftomed to meet in the fhade of the evening, and converfe upon a variety of fubjects; the young and vigorous divert themfelves with dances and other paftimes, and the children of different ages amufe themfelves with a thoufand fports and gambols adapted to their age: fome aim their little arrows at marks, or dart their light and blunted javelins at each other, to form themfelves for the exercifes of war and the chace; others wreftle naked upon the fand, or run in fportive races, with a degree of activity which I have never feen among the Europeans, who pretend to be our mafters.

I have defcribed to you the building of our houfes; fimple as they are, they anfwer every purpofe of human life, and every man is his own architect. An hundred or two of thefe edifices compofe our towns, which are generally furrounded by lofty hedges of thorns to fecure us from the midnight attacks of wild beafts, with only a fingle entrance, which is carefully clofed at night.

You talk, faid Tommy, of wild beafts; pray have you many of them in your country?

try? Yes, said the black, master, we have them of many sorts, equally dreadful and ferocious. First, we have the lion, which I dare say you have heard of, and perhaps seen. He is bigger than the largest mastiff, and infinitely stronger and more fierce; his paws alone are such, that with a single blow, he is able to knock down a man, and almost every other animal; but these paws are armed with claws so sharp and dreadful, that nothing can resist their violence. When he roars, every beast of the forest betakes himself to flight, and even the boldest hunter can scarcely hear it without dismay. Sometimes, the most valiant of our youth assemble in bands, arm themselves with arrows and javelins, and go to the chace of these destructive animals. When they have found his retreat, they generally make a circle round, uttering shouts and cries, and clashing their arms, to rouze him to resistance. The lion, mean-while, looks round upon his assailants with indifference or contempt; neither their number, nor their horrid shouts, nor the glitter of their radiant arms, can daunt him for an instant. At length he begins to lash his sides with his long and nervous tail, a certain sign of rising rage, his eyes sparkle with

with deftructive fires and, if the number of the hunters is very great, he perhaps moves flowly on. But this he is not permitted to do; a javelin, thrown at him from behind, wounds him in the flank, and compels him to turn. Then you behold him rouzed to fury and defperation; neither wounds, nor ftreaming blood, nor a triple row of barbed fpears, can prevent him from fpringing upon the daring black who has wounded him. Should he reach him, in the attack, it is certain death; but generally the hunter, who is at once contending for glory and his own life, and is inured to danger, avoids him by a nimble leap, and all his companions haften to his affiftance. Thus is the lion preffed and wounded on every fide, his rage is ineffectual, and only exhaufts his ftrength the fafter; an hundred wounds are pouring out his blood at once, and at length he bites the ground in the agonies of death, and yields the victory though unconquered.

When he is dead, he is carried back in triumph by the hunters, as a trophy of their courage. All the village rufhes out at once; the young, the old, women and children, uttering joyful fhouts, and praifing the valour of their champions. The elders

elders admire his prodigious fize, his mighty limbs, his dreadful fangs, and perhaps repeat tales of their own exploits; the women feem to tremble at their fierce enemy even in his death; while the men compel their children to approach the monfter, and tinge their little weapons in his blood. All utter joyful exclamations, and feafts are made in every houfe, to which the victors are invited as the principal guefts. Thefe are intended at once to reward thofe who have performed fo gallant an achievement, and to encourage a fpirit of enterprize in the reft of the nation.

What a dreadful kind of hunting muft this be, faid Tommy. But I fuppofe if any one meets a lion alone, it is impoffible to refift him. Not always, anfwered the black. I will tell you what I once was witnefs to myfelf. My father was reckoned not only the moft fkilful hunter, but one of the braveft of our tribe: innumerable are the wild beafts which have fallen beneath his arm. One evening, when the inhabitants of the whole village were affembled at their fports and dances, a monftrous lion, allured, I fuppofe, by the fmell of human flefh, burft unexpectedly upon them, without warning them of his approach, by roaring

ing as he commonly does. As they were unarmed, and unprepared for defence, all but my father inſtantly fled, trembling, to their huts; but he, who had never yet turned his back upon any beaſt of the foreſt, drew from his ſide a kind of knife, or dagger, which he conſtantly wore, and, placing one knee and one hand upon the ground, waited the approach of his terrible foe. The lion inſtantly ruſhed upon him with a fury not to be deſcribed; but my father received him upon the point of his weapon, with ſo ſteady and ſo compoſed an aim, that he buried it ſeveral inches in his belly. The beaſt attacked him a ſecond time, and a ſecond time received a dreadful wound, not however without laying bare one of my father's ſides with a ſudden ſtroke of his claws. The reſt of the village then ruſhed in, and ſoon diſpatched the lion with innumerable wounds.

This exploit appeared ſo extraordinary, that it ſpread my father's fame throughout the whole country, and gained him the name of the undaunted hunter, as an honourable diſtinction, from the neighbourhood.—Under ſuch a parent, it was not long before I was taught every ſpecies of the chace. At firſt, my father only ſuffered

fered me to purfue ftags and other feeble animals, or took me in his canoe to fifh. Soon, however, I was entrufted with a bow and arrows, and placed with many other children and young men to defend our ricefields from the depredations of the riverhorfe. Rice, it is neceffary to obferve, is a plant that requires great moifture in the foil; all our plantations, therefore, are made by the fide of rivers, in the foft fertile foil which is overflowed in the rainy feafon. But, when the grain is almoft ripe, we are forced to defend it from a variety of hurtful animals, that would otherwife deprive us of the fruits of our labours: among thefe, one of the principal is the animal I have mentioned. His fize and bulk are immenfe, being twice the bignefs of the largeft ox which I have feen in this country. He has four legs, which are fhort and thick, an head of a monftrous magnitude, and jaws that are armed with teeth of a prodigious fize and ftrength; befides two prominent tufks, which threaten deftruction to all affailants.

But this animal, though fo large and ftrong, is chiefly an inhabitant of the river, where he lives upon fifh and water-roots. It

It is sometimes a curious but a dreadful
fight, when a boat is gliding over a smooth
part of the stream, of unusual depth and
clearness, to look down and behold this
monstrous creature travelling along the
bottom several yards below the surface.
Whenever this happens, the boatman instantly paddles another way; for such is the
strength of the creature, that he is able to
overset a bark of moderate size, by rising
under it, or to tear out a plank with his
fangs, and expose those who are in it to the
dangers of an unexpected shipwreck. All
the day he chiefly hides himself in the water,
and preys upon fish; but, during the gloom
of night, he issues from the river, and invades the fields of standing corn, which he
would soon lay desolate, were he not driven
back by the shouts and cries of those who
are stationed to defend them. At this
work had I assisted several successive nights,
till we were almost wearied with watching.
At length, one of the most enterprizing of
our young men proposed, that we should no
longer content ourselves with driving back
the enemy, but boldly attack him, and punish him for his temerity. With this purpose, we concealed ourselves in a convenient spot, till we had seen one of the river-

horses

horses issue from the water, and advance a considerable way into our plantations: then we rushed from our hiding-place with furious shouts and cries, and endeavoured to intercept his return: but the beast, confiding in his superior strength, advanced slowly on, snarling horribly, and gnashing his dreadful tusks; and in this manner he opened his way through the thickest of our battalions. In vain we poured upon him on every side our darts and arrows, and every missive weapon; so well defended was he in an impenetrable hide, that every weapon either rebounded as from a wall, or glanced aside without in the least annoying. At length, one of the boldest of our youth advanced unguardedly upon him, and endeavoured to wound him from a shorter distance; but the furious beast, rushing upon him with an unexpected degree of swiftness, ripped up his body with a single stroke of his enormous tusks, and then, seizing him in his furious jaws, lifted up his mangled body as if in triumph, and crushed him into a bleeding and promiscuous mass. Fear instantly seized upon our company; all involuntarily retreated, and seemed inclined to quit the unequal combat; all but myself, who, enflamed with grief and rage,

for

for the loſs of my companion, determined either to revenge his death, or periſh in the attempt. Seeing, therefore, that it was in vain to attack him in the uſual manner, I choſe the ſharpeſt arrow, and fitted it to the bow-ſtring; then, with a cool, unterrified aim, obſerving the animal that moved nimbly on to the river, I diſcharged it full at his broad and glaring eye-ball with ſuch ſucceſs, that the barbed point penetrated even to his brain, and the monſter fell expiring to the ground.

This action, magnified beyond its deſerts, gained me univerſal applauſe throughout the hamlet: I was from that time looked upon as one of the moſt valiant and fortunate of our youth. The immenſe body of the monſter which I had ſlain was cut to pieces, and borne in triumph to the village. All the young women received me with ſongs of joy and congratulation; the young men adopted me as their leader in every hazardous expedition, and the elders applauded me with ſuch expreſſions of eſteem as filled my ignorant heart with vanity and exultation.

But what was more agreeable to me than all the reſt, my father received me with tranſport, and, preſſing me to his boſom

som with tears of joy, told me, that now he could die with pleasure, since I had exceeded his most sanguine expectations. I, said he, have not lived inactive, or inglorious; I have transfixed the tiger with my shafts; I have, though alone, attacked the lion in his rage, the terror of the woods, the fiercest of animals; even the elephant has been compelled to turn his back and fly before my javelin: but never, in the pride of my youth and strength, did I achieve such an exploit as this: He then went into his cabin and brought forth the bow and fatal arrows which he was accustomed to use in the chace. Take them, take them, said he, my son, and rescue my weaker arm from a burthen which it is no longer destined to sustain. Age is now creeping on; my blood begins to cool, my sinews slacken, and I am no longer equal to the task of supporting the glories of our race. That care shall now be thine, and with a firmer hand shalt thou henceforth use these weapons against the beasts of the forest and the enemies of our country.

Such was the account which the negro gave to Tommy, in different conversations, of of his birth and education. His curiosity was gratified with the recital, and his heart expanded in the same proportion that his knowledge improved. He reflected, with shame and contempt, upon the ridiculous prejudices he had once entertained; he learned to consider all men as his brethren and equals; and the foolish distinctions which pride had formerly suggested were gradually obliterated from his mind. Such a change in his sentiments rendered him more mild, more obliging, more engaging than ever; he became the delight of all the family; and Harry, although he had al ways loved him, now knew no limits to his affection.

One day he was surprized by an unexpected visit from his father, who met him with open arms, and told him, that he was now come to take him back to his own house. I have heard, said he, such an account of your present behaviour, that the past is intirely forgotten, and I begin to glory in owning you for a son. He then embraced him with the transports of an affectionate father who indulges the strongest sentiments of his heart, but sentiments he had long been forced to restrain. Tommy returned

returned his careffes with genuine warmth, but with a degree of refpect and humility he had once been little accuftomed to ufe. I will accompany you home, fir, faid he, with the greateft readinefs; for I wifh to fee my mother, and hope to give her fome fatisfaction of my future behaviour. You have both had too much to complain of in the paft; and I am unworthy of fuch affectionate parents. He then turned his face afide, and fhed a tear of real virtue and gratitude, which he inftantly wiped away as unworthy the compofure and fortitude of his new character..

But, fir, added he, I hope you will not object to my detaining you a little longer, while I return my acknowledgments to all the family, and take my leave of Harry. Surely, faid Mr. Merton, you can entertain no doubt upon that fubject: and, to give you every opportunity of difcharging all your duties to a family, to which you owe fo much, I intend to take a dinner with Mr. Sandford, whom I now fee coming home, and then returning with you in the evening.

At this inftant farmer Sandford approached, and very refpectfully faluting Mr. Merton, invited him to walk in. But L.6. Mr.

Mr. Merton, after returning his civility, drew him aside as if he had some private business to communicate. When they were alone, he made him every acknowledgement that gratitude could suggest; but words, added Mr. Merton, are very insufficient to return the favours I have received; for it is to your excellent family, together with the virtuous Mr. Barlow, that I owe the preservation of my son. Let me, therefore, intreat you to accept of what this pocket book contains, as a slight proof of my sentiments, and lay it out in whatever manner you please, for the advantage of your family.

Mr. Sandford, who was a man both of sense and humour, took the book, and, examining the inside, found that it contained bank-notes to the amount of some hundred pounds. He then carefully shut it up again, and, returning it to Mr. Merton, told him that he was infinitely obliged to him for the generosity which prompted him to such a princely act; but, as to the present itself, he must not be offended if he declined it. Mr. Merton, still more astonished at such disinterestedness, pressed him with every argument he could think of; he desired him to consider the state of his family;

family; his daughters unprovided for; his son himself, with difpofitions that might adorn a throne, brought up to labour; and his own advancing age, which demanded eafe and refpite, and an increafe of the conveniencies of life.

And what, replied the honeft farmer, is it, but thefe conveniencies of life, that are the ruin of all the nation? When I was a young man, Mafter Merton, and that is near forty years ago, people in my condition thought of nothing but doing their duty to God and man, and labouring hard: this brought down a bleffing upon their heads, and made them thrive in all their worldly concerns. When I was a boy, farmers did not lie droning in bed as they do now till fix or feven; my father, I believe, was as a good a judge of bufinefs as any in the neighbourhood, and turned as ftraight a furrow as any ploughman in the county of Devon; that filver cup, which I intend to have the honour of drinking your health out of to-day at dinner, that very cup was won by him at the great ploughing-match near Axminfter.—Well, my father ufed to fay, that a farmer was not worth a farthing that was not in the field by four; and my poor dear mother too, the beft-
tem-

tempered woman in the world, she always began milking exactly at five; and if a single soul was to be found in bed after four in summer, you might have heard her from one end of the farm to the other.—I would not disparage any body, or any thing, my good sir, but those were times indeed; the women, then, knew something about the management of an house: it really was quite a pleasure to hear my poor mother lecture the servants; and the men were men, indeed; pray, did you ever hear the story of my father's being at Truro, and throwing the famous Cornish wrestler, squinting Dick the miner?

Mr. Merton began to be convinced, that, whatever other qualities good Mr. Sandford might have, he did not excel in brevity; and therefore endeavoured in still stronger terms to overcome the delicacy of the farmer, and prevail upon him to accept his present.

But the good farmer pursued his point thus; Thank you, thank you, my dear sir, a thousand times, for your good will; but, as to the money, I must beg your pardon if I persist in refusing it. Formerly, sir, as I was saying, we were all happy and healthy, and our affairs prospered, because
we

we never thought about the conveniencies of life: now, I hear of nothing else. One neighbour, for I will not mention names, brings his fon up to go a fhooting with gentlemen; another fends his to market upon a blood horfe, with a plated bridle; and then the girls, the girls!—There is fine work, indeed; they muft have their hats and feathers, and riding-habits; their heads as big as buſhels, and even their hind-quarters ſtuck out with cork or paſteboard; but ſcarcely one of them can milk a cow, or churn, or bake, or do any one thing that is neceſſary in a family; ſo that unleſs the government will fend them all to this new ſettlement, which I have heard ſo much of, and bring us a cargo of plain, honeſt houſewives, who have never been at boarding-ſchools, I cannot conceive how we farmers are to get wives.

Mr. Merton laughed very heartily at this ſally, and told him, that he would venture to aſſert it was not ſo at his houſe.—Not quite ſo bad, indeed, ſaid the farmer; my wife was bred up under a notable mother, and, though ſhe muſt have her tea every afternoon, is, in the main, a very good ſort of woman. She has brought her daughters up a little better than uſual; but I can af-

ſure

sure you she and I have had many a good argument upon the subject. Not but she approves their milking, spinning, and making themselves useful; but she would fain have them genteel, Master Merton: all women now are mad after gentility; and, when once gentility begins, there is an end of industry. Now, were they to hear of such a sum as you have generously offered, there would be no peace in the house. My wenches, instead of Deb and Kate, would be Miss Deborah and Miss Catharine; in a little time, they must be sent to boarding-school, to learn French and music, and wriggling about the room. And, when they come back, who must boil the pot, or make the pudding, or sweep the house, or serve the pigs?—Did you ever hear of Miss Juliana, or Miss Harriet, or Miss Carolina, doing such vulgar things?

Mr. Merton was very much struck with the honest farmer's method of expressing himself, and could not help internally allowing the truth of his representations; yet he still pressed him to accept his present, and reminded him of the improvement of his farm.

Thank you again, and again, replied the farmer; but the whole generation of the Sandfords

Sandfords have been brought up to labour with their own hands for these hundred years; and, during all that time, there has not been a dishonest person, a gentleman, or a madman amongst us. And shall I be the first to break the customs of the family, and perhaps bring down a curse on all our heads?—What could I have more, if I were a lord, or a macaroni, as I think you call them?—I have plenty of victuals and work, good firing, cloaths, a warm house, a little for the poor, and, between you and I, something, perhaps, in a corner to set my children off with, if they behave well.— Ah! neighbour, neighbour, if you did but know the pleasure of holding plough after a good team of horses, and then going tired to bed, perhaps you'd wish to have been brought up a farmer too.—But in one word, as well as a thousand, I shall never forget the extraordinary kindness of your offer; but, if you would not ruin a whole family of innocent people that love you, even consent to leave us as we are.

Mr. Merton then seeing the fixed determination of the farmer, and feeling the justice of his coarse but strong morality, was obliged, however reluctantly, to desist;

fift; and Mrs. Sandford coming to invite them to dinner, he entered the houfe, and paid his refpects to the family.

After the cloth was removed, and Mr. Sandford had twice or thrice replenifhed his filver mug, the only piece of finery in his houfe, little Harry came running in, with fo much alacrity and heedleffnefs, that he tore Mifs Deborah's beft apron, and had nearly precipitated Mifs Catharine's new cap into the fire, for which the young ladies and his mother rebuked him with fome acrimony. But Harry, after begging pardon with his ufual good humour, cried, Father, father, here is the prettieft team of horfes, all matched, and of a colour, with new harnefs, the moft complete I ever faw in my life; and they have ftopped at our back-door, and the man fays they are brought for you. Farmer Sandford was juft then in the middle of his hiftory of the ploughing-match at Axminfter; but the relation of his fon had fuch an involuntary effect upon him, that he ftarted up, over-fet the liquor and the table, and, making an hafty apology to Mr. Merton, ran out to fee thefe wonderful horfes.

Prefently he returned, in equal admiration with his fon. Mafter Merton, faid he, I did

I did not think you had been so good a judge of an horse. I suppose they are a new purchase, which you want to have my opinion upon; and, I can assure you, they are the true Suffolk sorrels, the first breed of working horses in the kingdom; and these are some of the best of their kind. Such as they are, answered Mr. Merton, they are yours; and I cannot think, after the obligations I am under to your family, that you will do me so great a displeasure as to refuse. Mr. Sandford stood for some time in mute astonishment; but, at length, he was beginning the civilest speech he could think of to refuse so great a present, when Tommy coming up, took him by the hand, and begged him not to deny to his father and himself the first favour they had ever asked. Besides, said he, this present is less to yourself than to little Harry; and, surely, after having lived so long in your family, you will not turn me out with disgrace, as if I had misbehaved. —Here Harry himself interposed, and, considering less the value of the present than the feelings and intentions of the giver, he took his father by the hand, and besought him to oblige master Merton and his

his father. Were it any one elfe, I would not fay a word, added he; but I know the generofity of Mr. Merton, and the goodnefs of mafter Tommy fo well, that they will receive more pleafure from giving, than you from taking the horfes. Though I muft confefs, they are fuch as would do credit to any body; and they beat farmer Knowles's all to nothing, which have long been reckoned the beft team in all the country.

This laft reflection, joined with all that had preceded, overcame the delicacy of Mr. Sandford; and he at length confented to order the horfes to be led into his ftables. And now Mr. Merton, having made the moft affectionate acknowledgements to all this worthy and happy family, among whom he did not forget the honeft black, whom he promifed to provide for, fummoned his fon to accompany him home. Tommy arofe, and, with the fincereft gratitude, bade adieu to Harry and all the reft, I fhall not be long without you, faid he to Harry; to your example I owe moft of the little good that I can boaft; you have taught me how much better it is to be ufeful than rich or fine; how much more amiable

able to be good than to be great.—Should I be ever tempted to relapfe, even for an inftant, into any of my former habits, I will return hither for inftruction; and I hope you will again receive me. Saying this, he fhook his friend Harry affectionately by the hand, and, with watery eyes, accompanied his father home.

THE END.

LIST of BOOKS
PRINTED FOR J. STOCKDALE, PICCADILLY.

All the Books in this List are to be considered as being in Boards, unless otherwise expressed, and may be had on the shortest Notice from any of the Booksellers in Great Britain.

	£ s d
ABERCROMBIE's Hot-houfe Ga dener, royal 8vo.	0 6 0
———— Ditto, plates, coloured	0 8 6
———— Kitchen Gardener, 12mo.	0 4 0
———— Gardener's Calendar, 12mo.	0 4 0
———— Vade Mecum, 18mo.	0 3 6
Adams's Hiftory of Republics, 3 vols. 8vo.	1 1 0
Adventures of Numa Pompilius, 2 vols.	0 6 0
Æfop's Fables, with 112 plates, from Barlow's Defigns, 2 vols. elephant 8vo.	2 12 6
Ancient and Modern Univerfal Hiftory, 60 vols.	15 0 0
Ditto, calf, lettered	18 0 0
Andrew's Anecdotes, Ancient and Modern, 8vo.	0 7 6
———— Plans of Cities, 42 plates, with defcriptions, 4to. half bound	1 1 0
———— Ditto, with coloured plates, half-bound	2 2 0
Arms of the Peers and Peereffes of Great Britain, &c.	0 2 6
Arms of the Baronets of Great Britain	0 2 6
Arnold's Church Mufic, folio, half-bound	1 6 0
Ayfcough's Index to Shakefpeare, 8vo	0 18 0
———— Shakefpeare, with Index, 2 vols. 8vo.	1 11 6
———— Ditto, without Index, 1 vol. 8vo.	0 18 0
Barlow's Vifion of Columbus, 12mo.	0 2 6
Bayley on Mufic, Poetry, and Oratory, 8vo.	0 6 0
Beauties of the Britifh Senate, 2 vols. 8vo.	0 10 6
Berquin's Children's Friend, 6 vols. with 46 copper-plates	0 18 0
———— Ditto, 4 vols. 12mo.	0 8 0
———— Ditto, in French, with plates	0 12 0
———— Select Stories, 12mo.	0 2 6
Bonnet's Philofophical Inquiries, new edition, 8vo.	0 6 0
Bonnet on Chriftianity, 12mo.	0 2 6
Boothby's (Sir Brooke) Obfervations on Burke and Paine	0 5 0
Bofcawen's Horace, 8vo.	0 7 0
Briffot's Addrefs on the State of France, with Notes, and a Preface by the Tranflator	0 2 6
Broome's Elucidation of Haftings's Trial, 8vo.	0 5 0
Burke's Charges and Haftings's Anfwer, 8vo.	0 10 6
Cavendifh's State of Ireland, 8vo.	0 10 6
Chalmer's Collection of Treaties between Great Britain and other Powers, 2 vols.	0 15 0
———— Eftimate of the Comparative Strength of Great Britain, 8vo. boards	0 7 6
———— Life of Ruddiman, 8vo.	0 6 0
———— Life of de Foe, 8vo.	0 2 6
Champion on the American Commerce, 8vo.	0 5 0
Collection of Tracts on the Regency, 2 vols. 8vo.	1 10 0
Cooke's Voyage, 12mo. new edition, with plates	0 3 6

LIST OF BOOKS.

	£	s.	d.
Davis's Historical Tracts, with his Life, 8vo. by George Chalmers, F. R. S. S. A.	0	5	0
Day's Dying Negro, new edition, 8vo. with a frontispiece by Mentz and Neagle	0	3	0
—— History of Sandford and Merton, 3 vols.	0	9	0
—— Ditto, in 1 vol. frontispiece, by Stothard	0	3	6
—— Tracts, including the Dying Negro, 8vo.	0	13	6
—— Children's Miscellany	0	3	0
—— History of Sandford and Merton, 2 vols. (French)	0	6	0
Debates in Parliament, (Stockdale's) from 1784 to 1792 inclusive, 21 vols. 8vo. half-bound, uncut	8	8	0
De Foe's History of the Union, 4to.	1	10	0
Dobson's Petrarch's View of Human Life, 8vo.	0	6	0
Edwards's History of the West Indies, 2 vols. 4to. with maps and historical plates	2	12	6
—— Ditto, fine paper	3	3	0
The maps and historical plates, separate, 4to.	0	10	6
Fielding's New Peerage of England, Scotland, and Ireland	0	6	0
Filson's History of Kentucky, with a large map, 19 inches by 17	0	2	0
Fleurieu's Voyages and Discoveries of the French, 4to.	1	1	0
Gay's Fables, (Stockdale's edition) 2 vols. elephant, 8vo. with 70 plates	1	11	6
Gordon's (Sir Adam) Contrast, 2 vols. 12mo.	0	6	0
—————— Selection of Psalms	0	1	6
—————— Homilies of the Church of England, 2 vols. 8vo.	0	14	0
Hawkins's History of the Ottoman Empire, 4 vols.	1	6	0
Hill's Travels through Sicily and Calabria in 1791, royal 8vo.	0	7	6
History of the Regency, 8vo.	0	10	6
History of New Holland, 8vo. with maps	0	6	0
Holt's Characters of Kings, with frontispiece by Mentz	0	3	0
Hunter's Voyages in the South Seas, with 17 plates, 4to.	1	11	6
—— Historical Journal Abridged, 8vo.	0	7	6
Jackson's Constitution of the American States, 8vo.	0	6	0
Jefferson's History of Virginia, 8vo.	0	7	0
Indian Vocabulary	0	3	6
Johnson's Works, vol. 12 and 13, containing his Debates in Parliament	0	12	0
Latrobe's Anecdotes of the Kings of Prussia, 8vo.	0	6	0
———— History of Struenzee and Brandt	0	4	0
———— History of the Moravian Missions in America	0	8	6
Law on the Rising Resources of India, royal 8vo.	0	6	0
Life of Dante and Petrarch	0	2	6
List of Militia Officers, with the Dates of their Commissions, &c.	0	2	6
London Calendar Complete, for 1795, bound	0	9	6
———— in morocco extra, with gilt edges	0	14	6
———— single, bound	0	2	6

LIST OF BOOKS.

	£	s.	d.
London Calendar complete, and Almanack, bound	0	3	6
Lloyd's (General) Defence of England	0	5	0
Morse's History of America, 4to. with 25 Maps	1	6	0
———— American Geography, 8vo. with maps	0	6	6
———— fine paper, with coloured maps	0	8	6
———— Ditto, abridged, with eight plates, bound	0	3	6
New Robinson Crusoe, 2 vols. 12mo. 32 cuts	0	6	0
———————————— in 1 vol. 12mo. 32 cuts	0	3	6
———————————— abridged, in 1 vol. 12mo. 32 cuts, bound	0	2	6
Parliamentary Guide, 8vo	0	7	0
Perry's New General English Pocket Dictionary	0	3	6
———— New Standard French and English Pronouncing Dictionary	0	4	0
Philips's Voyage to Botany Bay, with 55 plates, 4to	1	11	6
———————— with coloured plates	2	12	6
———————— third edition, 8vo. with 20 plates	0	10	6
Playfair's Commercial and Political Atlas, with 44 plates	1	1	0
Pye's Commentary of Aristotle, royal 4to.	1	6	0
———— Poems on various Subjects, 2 vols. 8vo.	0	12	0
———— Poetic of Aristotle	0	4	0
———— Spectre, a Novel, 2 vols.	0	6	0
———— Amusement	0	2	6
———— Observations on Hunting, with Frontispiece and Vignette, by Stothard and Heath	0	6	0
Ramsay's History of the American War, 2 vols. 8vo.	0	12	0
Robinson Crusoe, 2 vols. Demy Octavo, with 17 plates (Stockdale's Edition)	0	18	0
Rouse on the landed Property of Bengal, 8vo.	0	6	0
Sayer's Lindor and Adelaide, 12mo.	0	3	6
Scott's History of the East Indies, 2 vols. 4to.	2	2	0
Seally's Geographical Dictionary, 2 vols. 4to. half-bound	1	11	6
Short Review of the British Government in India	0	3	6
Simkin's Humorous and Satirical Letters, complete, 8vo.	0	7	0
Sketch of Universal History, with 36 heads of kings	0	1	6
Smith on the Human Species, 8vo.	0	2	6
Stockdale's Trial for a supposed Libel, royal 8vo.	0	5	0
Thomson's Seasons, with 14 plates, by Stothard, elegantly printed on a superfine wove paper, (Stockdale's edition)	0	9	0
Wallace's New Book of Interest, half bound	0	10	6
Whitaker's History of Arianism, 2 vols. royal 8vo.	0	10	6
———————— Course of Hannibal, 2 vols. 8vo.	0	12	0
Wray's Resolves of the Gloucester Committee, 8vo.	0	4	0
Zelia in the Desert, or the Female Robinson Crusoe	0	2	6
Berquin's Honest Farmer, with frontispiece	0	1	0
———————— History of Little Grandison	0	1	0
Day's History of Little Jack, with 23 cuts	0	1	0
Gordon's (Sir Adam) Affectionate Advice	0	1	0
The History of the School Boy, with cuts	0	1	0

www.ingramcontent.com/pod-product-compliance
Lightning Source LLC
Chambersburg PA
CBHW031348230426
43670CB00006B/471